AFFIRMATIONS 101

101 Days of Developing Self-confidence, Boldness and Courage While Turning Dreams Into Reality.

CARLY —
a great way to
start your day —
with an affirmation!
Read intro first
and read affirmations
aloud so you
hear the
words!!

JACOB GLASS

XO
Pamela

DEDICATION:

For my beloved students and practitioners across the world and for dear Vetura Papke, the practitioner of practitioners.

INTRODUCTION

I love for things to be simple and this may be the simplest book I have written so far. Please use this book in the way that you find most helpful. It is designed to read from beginning to end, with one affirmation per day, read in the morning, to set the tone for your day.

However, you may choose to simply "plop" it open each day and take whatever affirmation is on that page. That day's affirmation is the first line of each page – after that is a brief essay and then usually an affirmative statement to more deeply ground the affirmation in your mind.

I do <u>suggest</u> that you do only one affirmation per day on your first time through. It is also EXTREMELY helpful and effective if you write out the affirmation 5 times so that it begins to seep into your subconscious mind (you may want to shorten some of the longer affirmations if it helps). In addition, I strongly urge you to SPEAK the affirmation out loud 3 times slowly and with feeling. Feel free to change the wording until it fits and feels like "you." And remember, this is meant to be fun so use the book that is the most enjoyable way for YOU! You may even want to cut out the pages and tape them on your bathroom mirror. Be free, have fun!

(Where you see "ACIM" after a quote, it stands for A Course in Miracles.)

EPIGRAPH

"Every word we speak and every thought we think is an affirmation."

- Louise L. Hay

ACKNOWLEDGMENTS

Dear everyone, I love you and this book is for you.

AFFIRMATIONS 101

Affirmation 1

I Activate the Peace of God Within Myself.

"I want the peace of God. To say these words is nothing. But to mean these words is everything." - ACIM

Life is responding to the energy that is active within us. No one else is thinking in our minds and so we are free to choose what we will focus on each day, and each moment. We can decide right now to devote the remainder of this year to joyful expansion, grateful moments, savoring the present and a happy journey into the future – remembering that a year is made up of the choices we make each day. If we refuse to let ourselves be swayed by the voices of fear today, we can have a day of limitless love, abundant good and deep inner peace.

Decide now the kind of day you want to have – how you want to feel and the energy that you want to bring to all that you do or experience. Set a positive intention and know that the Universe is a friendly Force that responds to us by reflecting back to us our thoughts and feelings.

There is a Power and Presence for good in the Universe and I call upon It today to guide me into my greatest good so far. There is nothing holding me back and I walk in joyful love today as I practice thinking thoughts that feel good.

AFFIRMATION 2

I AM ALWAYS AT THE RIGHT PLACE AT THE RIGHT TIME.

"You may think this implies that an enormous amount of time is necessary . . . but let me remind you that time and space are under my control." -ACIM

THE UNIVERSE HAS PERFECT TIMING. To be *"in the right place at the right time"* means that we are present in the here and now instead of clinging to the past or projecting into the future. There is no need to worry or rush. Our impending good will meet us down the road if we will stay on track. Today contains all the blessings, resources, people and opportunities for our greater good if we are calm and open enough to see them as they present themselves.

Rushing around frantically trying to make things happen actually interferes with the effortless unfolding of today's good. As we relax, become still inside and connect with Source, we find that everything is held perfectly in the hands of God and all we need to do is align ourselves with the Divine Presence – even in the midst of a very busy day.

I am open to receive the gifts of this day. I need do nothing to deserve or earn them for they are gifts waiting for me to recognize and open them. I am calm and present knowing that right here and now, everything is coming to me in perfect Divine Order and timing.

AFFIRMATION 3

THERE IS INFINITE POWER IN MY SPOKEN WORD.

"Your word is your wand." – FLORENCE SCOVEL SCHINN

IN THE BOOK OF GENESIS, GOD SPEAKS THE WORLD into existence – *"let there be light, let there be firmament"* and so on. And since we are extensions of God, we too have the power to speak our world into existence every day. We have been given dominion over the Earth and yet many of us live as if the world has dominion over us.

Today we can begin to take back our power by consciously choosing the words that we speak. Much of what we think of as truth or factual is really nothing more than a limiting belief that we are speaking into our reality.

We may say, *"no one is hiring people like me anymore"* thinking that this is just the way of it. We don't realize that all we've done is affirm a limiting belief that we heard somewhere. In reality, there is a very good chance that somewhere someone "like you" IS being hired at this very moment – because they were holding a different belief than you are. They may not even be as qualified as you are, but they DO have a different set of beliefs.

The real "glass ceiling" in life is not put there by the world but by our own Consciousness and by what we believe is possible for us. The words we speak are like a magic wand that creates for us whatever we are speaking into the Divine Mind. Speak positively and consciously today.

I am a co-creator with the Divine Mind today and I am excited to create a day of limitless possibilities for my good. The only limits for me are set by my own imagination.

AFFIRMATION 4

GOD IS WITH ME NOW. THERE IS A PLAN FOR MY LIFE.

*"For remembering Him means you are not alone,
and are willing to remember it."* -ACIM

WE ARE NOT ALONE on the journey through this day or through this life. Within and surrounding us is the Divine Source of all. In It we live, and move, and have our being. Nothing that we do or fail to do can separate us from this Source. We can choose to ignore or deny this Source and then FEEL separate, but the feeling is not a fact.

Our days are not at random - they are led by the guide we choose for our day. We can be guided by the small separate human mind of fear and limitation or we can be Guided by a Source that loves us beyond reason and without limit. This Source is not something outside of us pulling strings as if we were puppets. It is a Force that responds to our thoughts, feelings, words, and attitudes. We activate it positively or negatively by the way that we focus our attention.

The Divine Plan for our day is based on increasing our joy and happiness even when unexpected things happen and we are thrown off schedule. As we affirm the Divine Plan and the Divine Presence, we find that we are living in a state of joyously effortless accomplishment of good.

God is with me now. I am not alone. There is a perfect joyous Divine Plan for my life today and I relax into it now. I trust that the Power that holds galaxies in place can handle the details of my life. I expect a day of gently unfolding good as I remember that I am not alone.

AFFIRMATION 5

I BELIEVE IN THE POWER OF SOURCE WITHIN ME.

*"You are free to believe what you choose,
and what you do attests to what you believe."* - ACIM

WHAT DO YOU REALLY BELIEVE is possible for you? What do you believe life is? Do you believe that life is for or against you? Are you aware of all of your beliefs – even the ones that are not so obvious? Is it possible that you have some old hidden beliefs that are no longer serving you or are holding you back from getting more out of life?

Many people spend years reading spiritual books without really activating the principles in their own lives. And one of the first and most powerful ways we activate a principle is through our BELIEF. Wishing and hoping have no real power in them. We may want spiritual principle to be true for us, but wanting and believing are still very far apart. It is the power of the beliefs that we are activating daily that transform our lives, for the better or for the worse.

Let's begin this time together by activating the beliefs that serve us in dissolving our old limiting thoughts and beliefs. You may want to sit down at some point and write out the old beliefs you are releasing, as well as a list of the beliefs that are already serving you well - and then make a list of empowering new beliefs that will keep you aligned with your greater good.

I am dissolving old negative beliefs and replacing them with new empowering thoughts that help me live more fully and joyously. I believe that the best is yet to come!

AFFIRMATION 6

I BELIEVE IN THE RADICAL ACTION OF GOD'S LOVE HERE ON EARTH THROUGH ME.

*"Yet the real world has the power to touch you even here,
because you love it. And what you call with love
will come to you."* –ACIM

A FAR AWAY GOD IN THE SKY, or a spiritual happiness that does not kick-in until the after-life is a rather impotent belief system. The life of the Urban Mystic is one of direct contact with Infinite Wisdom and Divine Presence here and now.

When we look around and see a world devoid of love and Divinity it is not because It is not available or that It does not exist. It's that it has not been activated. It is like electricity in that sense – you cannot see it unless a connection is made and the power it activated. If you walk into a room that is dark, you don't pray that electricity will light the room for you. You plug in the lamp and activate the electricity by turning the switch on the lamp. It's a co-creative endeavor.

If we want an atmosphere of radical Divine Love in our lives, then we must activate it by getting plugged into the Source and drawing the Power through us into our environment. We are literally made of stardust and were expertly designed to be the Light of the world. Shine brightly today by demonstrating love for self and others in thoughts, words and deeds.

Today I will channel the Light of Love by activating it in myself. As I activate this Light within myself, it fills the space around me and illuminates my world with Love and Grace.

AFFIRMATION 7

THERE IS LIMITLESS GOOD –
MORE THAN ENOUGH FOR EVERYONE.

"To the Holy Spirit it is the law of extension. To the ego it is the law of deprivation. It therefore produces abundance or scarcity, depending on how you choose to apply it." -ACIM

WHEN WE ARE SPIRITUALLY ALIGNED, the good that we choose and accept for ourselves does not deplete the supply nor take from another. We are living in a Universe that is ever-expanding and creating more from out of the ethers. The Cosmic Source is not saying, *"I'd love to pay you more but I don't have it this month."* There is no shortage, and no diminishing resources when we turn to the ultimate Source.

We are meant to have an increasing abundance of all that is good – time, energy, health, love, friendship, kindness, talent, inspiration, money, opportunities, healing, resources, guidance, homes, transportation, ideas, and knowledge.

We all go through phases when the tide goes out and we have a season of apparent loss. This too is part of the natural cycle of abundance. Every night ends with morning, every winter turns to spring, and every storm passes in due season. These are the times to remember, *"fear not, be not afraid"* for if we will stay in faithful calm expectancy, soon enough the tide will turn and we will be swimming with the dolphins.

Today I open the portals of my soul to receive the abundant gifts of God as I relax into the Divine Flow of joyful living.

AFFIRMATION 8

LOTS CAN HAPPEN!

"To God all things are possible." -ACIM

THE EGO MIND THINKS IN TERMS OF FINITE RESOURCES, limitations and extremes. Black-and-white, all-or-nothing thinking dominates the fearful mind. *"Either I'll get this job, or I'll lose everything and end up on the streets"* is the kind of fearful attached thinking that keeps us stressed out and depressed.

Divine thinking is expansive and limitless. Our part is <u>not</u> figuring out HOW our manifestation will happen – our part is to be miracle-minded and openhearted. When the situation seems hopeless or when we see few or even no options, we can remember that with God all things are possible. We must not limit the Divine Force but instead can remember that Spirit knows of ways that are as yet unknown to us. We do not have to design the recipe or draw the blueprint in these situations. There is a Power in us that sees a much bigger picture than we possibly could.

It can be very helpful at times for us to relax into a very general kind of affirmation that gives us more breathing space. When we remind ourselves that *"lots can happen"* we are activating our faith muscle and letting go of fearfully trying to micromanage people and situations. As we relax we are able to open our valve to receive and channel more good.

I will not limit my possibilities with either/or thinking today but will remember that "lots can happen" when it comes to the doors leading to my greater good.

AFFIRMATION 9

I AM NOT LIMITED BY MY PAST.

"The past is over. It can touch me not." -ACIM

THE UNIVERSE IS READY TO START OVER AGAIN every moment. In the Cosmic Order there is no need for us to "suffer" for our mistakes, for time and space are only man-made concepts. It is only by holding onto our mistakes and feelings of guilt that we delay our progress. If we are willing to *learn* from our mistakes, clean up our mess, apologize and let it go, then Spirit can "cancel the debt" for us. This is what "forgive" means – the debt is cancelled.

This past is not only what happened in our childhood, or last year - even the mistake that just happened a few minutes ago can be dissolved in a moment of Grace. Grace is available to us at any moment in which we are humble enough to let go of defending our mistakes, to stop justifying our attacks and defensiveness, and to release the idea that restoration will take time. Spirit is not time-bound and miracles happen in the NOW.

I now surrender all mistakes and errors of my past to the Holy Spirit within me to be dissolved. I let go of guilt and the projection of guilt as I now breathe in the peace of God. I choose to grow in love, joy and wisdom from all situations and I ask Spirit to reveal to me if there is anything I need to do or not do. I am willing to learn and grow from this experience.

AFFIRMATION 10

MY BEST YEARS ARE STILL AHEAD OF ME.

*"The purpose of time is to enable you to learn
how to use time constructively."* -ACIM

WHETHER YOU ARE 25 OR 85 you can believe that the best is yet to come for you. Each one of us has a future that we can look forward to with enthusiasm, regardless of the chronological age of our body. Life tends to reflect back to us our own attitudes and thoughts.

Perhaps we've slowed down or have physical challenges or limitations, but that is no reason to begin to withdraw from life and start sitting on the bench. The game of Life will meet us where we are today. Our physical "best" often changes from day to day – so what? Monday we may have high energy, less on Tuesday and then be reinvigorated by Thursday, but let's not attach a story of age to the ups and downs of the body.

There are people who are getting married to the love of their life at 90, starting a new business at 70, writing their first book at 80, and adopting a child at 60. Let's not judge according to something as meaningless as the age of our physical vessel. It's not too late. We can always dream new dreams.

I am happy in my now and looking forward to what is yet to come. There is nothing to stop me but a silly story about age. I choose to live in a world that is dominated by joy rather than by time or numbers. I choose to let go of limited thinking and believe that there is much good yet to come.

AFFIRMATION 11

MY VALVE IS WIDE OPEN.

"A healed mind is relieved of the belief that it must plan." -
ACIM

WE DO NOT NEED TO GO OUT to conquer the world today.
There is no one to fight against and nothing is withholding
our good from us. In fact, a "get" mentality is usually not
always the most receptive mentality. Energetically, we want
to focus more on the idea of receiving than getting.

When we think in terms of receiving, there is a feeling of
loving partnership with the Universe. This allows us to relax
and soften. The idea of getting tends to put us in opposition –
it's almost like we're trying to rob or take something away
from someone or something else. And since the Universe
mirrors our energy back to us, if we are trying to "get from"
then we are setting up a momentum in which others will be
"getting" from us.

If we simply shift that energy to being open to receive the
blessings and good of the Universe, we've softened our
hearts and opened our minds to be more alert and receptive
to guidance. Think in terms of an energetic valve that you
are opening in order to let the good flow to and through you.

*I am in tune with the Infinite Source of all that is good. I let
go of scheming and strategizing and align myself with the
wisdom and guidance of Source to guide me to all the right
people, places and situations for the greatest good of all
concerned today. I am open, open, open.*

Affirmation 12

I Decide How I Want to Feel Today.

"The power of decision is my own." - ACIM

Feelings are just feelings. They are not good or bad, appropriate or inappropriate. They just are. And though they can be extremely powerful, we are not powerless to change them. We can learn how to gradually take charge of our emotions and work with them rather than fighting against them or surrendering to them.

Of course, going from deeply depressed to a state of elated joy is far too huge a jump to make in one leap. Instead, when we do not like the way we are feeling, it is much better to start to move in a direction that just brings a little more breathing space than where we currently are. We are looking for progress, not perfection.

We can change the way we feel gently and kindly by admitting where we are and choosing to move in a new direction with God's help. If you do not like the way you are feeling today, try the prayer below:

Beloved Infinite Spirit, I do not like the feelings I have right now and I want to be healed. I let go of attachment to any painful stories or limiting thoughts that are supporting these feelings and I ask that You guide me to greater wisdom and understanding regarding my thinking and the situations in my life. I want to feel _____ and _____ and I now surrender these goals to You that I may be returned to sanity, joy and inner peace through Your Grace. Thank You. - Amen.

AFFIRMATION 13

I LOOK FOR AND FIND THE GOOD IN MY WORLD.

"I rule my mind, which I alone must rule." - ACIM

MIND IS A POWERFUL SERVANT — it will begin to gather up evidence that we are right no matter what we believe. It can gather up evidence that we are worthless garbage and that no one loves us. And it can just as easily make a case that we are adored as the Light of the world.

Whatever we are unconsciously looking for, we will tend to find. We may be intently seeking love and partnership, but if we have a subconscious thought that we do not deserve love or that relationships are painful, then we will keep finding rejection, betrayal, loss and so on. Mind will gather up the evidence and bring it right through the front door if necessary.

Anytime you notice that you are having a critical or harsh thought about yourself, your world, or life, simply stop, take a breath and release it as it dissolves back into nothingness. Then, CHOOSE a new supportive thought. Don't make it difficult — make it FUN. It's actually exciting to discover an old limiting belief and then turning it around to a NEW more helpful thought because it FEELS so good!

I have a wonderful mind, which supports me in whatever I believe about life and myself. I choose now to direct my mind to gather up evidence of the good in myself, the good in others, and the good in my world.

Affirmation 14

I Am Walking Through the Open Doors.

*"Any direction that would lead you where the
Holy Spirit leads you not, goes nowhere."* -ACIM

How many times have we hurt ourselves smashing up against the doors that have kept us locked out? I cannot tell you the tremendous energy I wasted in my past trying to be a part of things that wanted no part of me. Finally, I called off the search, brought in the dogs, cancelled the auditioning for roles in life, and resigned from the race – and that is when doors began to open for me.

In our society we sometimes have a difficult time allowing life to be simple and even effortless. We've based so much of our history on pushing and conquering. We build statues to those who have fought the hardest and struggled the most.

There is another way. It is the way of the Divine Feminine within us. Yes, there are times for pushing but those times are extremely rare. Think of our species. For nine months there is relaxing into the natural order and allowing everything to be done without interference. Then, labor begins, and even all through labor the mother is told not to push until the very end of the process. That is a lot of time growing new life and only a very small amount of time pushing – something to think about.

I trust the process of Life and I am walking through the open doors to my greater good. I only want what wants me and we are a beautiful match!

AFFIRMATION 15

I SURRENDER TO GRACE KNOWING THAT GOD IS ON THE FIELD.

"God is in everything I see
because God is in my mind." -ACIM

AMERICAN MYSTIC AND AUTHOR JOEL S. GOLDSMITH would go into meditation just until he felt the inner "click" which to him signified that *"God is on the field."* At that moment he knew that he'd his sense of separate humanness out of the way and that the Divine Presence was now dominant. Healing had taken place on the inner planes even if it had not yet manifested in the physical. He was surrendering any remnants of trying to figure everything out by himself and was passing the ball to the Infinite Friend.

When we do this, we are not bringing the Divine to a place where It had been absent. We are shifting our attention away from focus on the problem to focus on the Answer. God has not moved - we've simply awakened to the Presence that was here all along. We've surrendered to Source.

All fear and anxiety dissolves now as I remember and acknowledge that God is on the field. I release struggling with my problems and choose to let Spirit lead the way.

AFFIRMATION 16

THEY'VE GOT THIS.

*"The alertness of the ego to the errors of others egos
is not the kind of vigilance the Holy Spirit
would have you maintain."* - ACIM

SEVERAL YEARS AGO I WAS STUCK in judgment of a public person because of a behavior that I thought was "unacceptable." I felt he was lying to his family and the public. I was suffering because instead of keeping my eyes on my own paper, I was policing the Universe and paying attention to things that were none of my business.

So, I asked Spirit to heal my mind of these attack thoughts. It's not that I wanted to be spiritual - I just wanted to stop suffering from these thoughts.

I was walking down the street less than an hour later when unexpectedly I saw the man I was judging sitting at a sidewalk café having lunch. Suddenly, in my inner vision I saw Jesus standing behind the man and He held up his hands and said to me, *"I've got this!"* That was my miracle. In that very instant I was able to let it go and drop my attack thoughts entirely. I've got splinters in my own eye.

My peace was returned and I felt wonderful. Later that very same day I discovered that the man had already come clean to his family about his behavior weeks before I even found out what he'd been up to. We waste energy and time when we are trying to be the moral authority of the Universe.

I let God be God as I step back and release everyone to their own perfect path of learning. I stay in my own business.

AFFIRMATION 17

MY RELATIONSHIPS ARE LOVING & HARMONIOUS.

*"If you point out the errors of your brother's ego
you must be seeing through yours, because the Holy Spirit
does not perceive his errors."* -ACIM

IF WE WANT TO HAVE HARMONIOUS relationships, whether personal or professional, we must focus on the positive aspects of the individuals and of the relationship.

When we begin finding fault in others, or in any relationship, we are activating a vibration that tears down rather than builds up. Whatever we focus on, we get more of in life. As we begin to pay attention to the errors and faults of others, those errors and faults will begin to become huge in our consciousness. Soon enough, nothing that they do is right or good enough for us. But, we are also capable of turning that mental habit pattern of judgment around very quickly if we are willing.

If there is someone in your life who is bothering you, try making a list of the "positive aspects" of that person and of the relationship. Whether this person is a mate, your child, a neighbor, relative, co-worker, or even a person in the news, you can begin to shift your own energy by choosing to look for and amplify ANY positive aspects you can possible find about this person, or about the relationship.

I choose to focus on the good in all those I interact with or think of today. I know that as I focus on the positive, my mind and heart begin to feel more spacious and I am able to allow more joy into my world.

AFFIRMATION 18

JOY IS THE COMPELLING FORCE IN MY WORLD.

*"There is no difference between love and joy. Therefore,
the only possible whole state is the wholly joyous."* - ACIM

NEVER UNDERESTIMATE THE POWER OF JOY to shift your attitude, your world, your life, and your world into a greater level of success.

Sometimes in my classes, during the guided meditation, I will say to the audience, *"What brings you joy? What makes your heart sing?"* And this immediately shifts the vibration of the room and opens a greater portal for Spirit to enter through. In fact, the word joy has a higher vibration even than the word love. Often when we say love, we are really talking about attachment and sentimentality. It's amazing the horrible things that have happened in this world in the name of love.

Joy is far less confusing and is actually the same thing as true spiritual love because it is free of the ego attachments. This joy is not frivolous or shallow. Any spiritual teaching that does not have joy at the core has shut God out.

I have a friend who finds great joy in working with grief and the dying. It makes his heart sing and fulfills a deep desire in him to be truly helpful. Again, joy is not silly or frivolous – it is the deepest of the deep.

My joy is a God-given gift that reveals to me where I am to go, what I am to do, what I am to say, and to whom. Joy leads me to all the right people and places for the greatest mutual benefit. Joy is my internal GPS.

AFFIRMATION 19

I BOLDLY MAKE GOOD CHOICES.

"As you decide so will you see.
And all that you see but witnesses to your decision." -ACIM

WISHING AND HOPING ARE LOW FREQUENCY vibrations, which means that they have very little magnetic power for Law of Attraction to work with. Being wishy-washy and timid about the life we want offers very little power in terms of manifestation and far too many spiritual types are afraid of their own power.

This boldness has nothing to do with being pushy, or being too stubborn to admit when we are wrong. In fact, what makes us able to make good choices is usually having experience with making some not-so-good choices along the way. But if we live in fear of making choices or are timid because we're afraid of making a mistake – well, we have not given the Universe anything to work with at all. WE MUST SOW A SEED for the Universe to act upon. The seed is our DECISION.

Instead of wishing and hoping, practice deciding and choosing. Make bold choices and stay open to guidance and correction as you go. Then watch Life respond!

I've decided to be happy! I've decided to let go of the past. I've decided to go for my dreams. I've decided to let in more love than I ever have before. I've decided to prosper and thrive. I've decided that I deserve to succeed in life. I've decided to open my heart. I've decided to step up my game. I've decided to ask for what I want and to play full out!

Affirmation 20

Wonderful People Are Drawn to Me and We Assist Each Other in Truly Helpful Ways.

*"What you perceive in others you
are strengthening in yourself."* - ACIM

Whatever we believe in our hearts & minds about people will tend to be reflected back to us rather quickly in our external world. We waste a lot of time and energy trying to change people when the real miraculous alchemy takes place when we change our MINDS about people and about ourselves.

Start by knowing that there is something wonderful about you and that you deserve all kinds of loving companionship – in business, friendships, romance, family, and in your community. Know that these relationships will be mutually beneficial and enjoyable. Affirm that you bring out the best in one another and that you live in a Consciousness of win-win.

Refuse to hold a grudge. Refuse to be offended. Refuse to close your heart. Simply realize that not everyone is going to like you or be a vibrational match to you. Let go easily and with Grace knowing that you will meet those whom you will resonate best with and that only good lies before you.

I honor my relationships with gratitude and appreciation and I know that the ideal companions are drawn to me without struggle. Law of Attraction is bringing to me those who are a match to the joy, peace and love that are flowing from my Consciousness today.

AFFIRMATION 21

ALL THE ANSWERS I NEED COME TO ME WITH EASE.

"In quietness are all things answered,
and is every problem quietly resolved." -ACIM

WE ARE CONNECTED TO INFINITE WISDOM – in fact, we are ONE with Infinite Wisdom. It's not up to us to figure everything out. All that is necessary is for us to tap into the Cosmic Source that is equally available to us all.

Right now, this very moment, let your shoulders drop, unclench your jaw, relax your eyes and all the muscles of the face and head, let your thoughts slow down, take a deep breath and let your heart open to receive . . . now, let all tension and stress drain from your fingertips and out the soles of your feet like sand through and hourglass. Know that there is nothing for you to fix, or change, nothing to figure out right now, nothing to grab hold of, and nothing to push away. Let there be nothing but this openness to receive as you relax and breathe, relax and breathe.

Right here, right now, there is nothing for me to do but receive. There is nothing to "get" or fix or change – just this gentle opening to receive what Spirit pours into and through me today. I am relaxed and receptive to the good that comes to me today.

AFFIRMATION 22

I ACCEPT MYSELF EXACTLY AS I AM.

*"The truth about you is so lofty that
nothing unworthy of God is worthy of you."* -ACIM

I WASTED SO MUCH TIME AND ENERGY trying to change myself into something or someone different. And any changes I ever made did not last for long.

I tried so hard to be a nicer person, a more spiritual person, to be sweeter, less opinionated, more social and outgoing, more affectionate, thinner, more muscular, and on and on – and all to no avail.

My awakening came when finally in one of my sessions of whining to Spirit about how I was just a horrible person who was incapable of change I heard that still small Voice of Inner Being within me say, *"I never asked you to be any different than you are. That was YOUR idea, not Mine. And I'm not going to help you make a change that I don't think is necessary or even helpful. I needed a YOU, not a watered-down version of someone else, so stop complaining to me. I see no problem here."* Wow. What a relief!

And the amazing miracle of learning to accept myself just as I am is that the more I do it, the more positive changes take place in me without waging a war against myself.

I am willing to change my mind about myself and if anything about me needs to be changed, I leave it to God to gently make those changes as I open to Divine Guidance and Wisdom.

AFFIRMATION 23

AFFIRM – BELIEVE – RELAX - RECEIVE.

*"Miracles are affirmations of Sonship,
which is a state of completion and abundance."* -ACIM

WE WANT OUR AFFIRMATIONS TO be life giving, soothing, uplifting, and helpful. They don't have to be the most amazing positive thoughts in the world – but they do need to go in a loving positive direction.

The next step is to BELIEVE what we are affirming instead of spending the rest of the day invalidating our affirmations. This means getting behind the affirmation instead of opposing it or doubting. Do this very gently – and it is much easier to do if our affirmations are more general, less specific, and more open. *"I am opening up to more financial abundance and having enough to share and to spare"* is usually easier to believe in than something as specific as, *"I have tripled my income this month"* – but only YOU know what is believable for you.

Then comes perhaps the most challenging part – RELAX. We are not trying to FORCE or make anything happen anymore than we would try to force the seed we planted in the ground to start to sprout. This is a cooperative process. We don't MAKE gravity work –we intelligently cooperate with the law. Our mental work is no different.

Then, we open to receive the harvest of our new thoughts once they begin to bear fruit. This sounds very simple, but it is somewhat surprising how many people who actually WANT to receive are not yet open enough to accept the good when it comes. Practice being a gracious receiver.

AFFIRMATION 24

I AM A UNIQUE BEING. I DON'T NEED TO FIT IN.

"For this world is the opposite of Heaven . . .
and everything here takes a direction exactly
opposite of what is true." -ACIM

I'VE BEEN QUITTING my whole life. I am not only a college dropout; I quit kindergarten after one day! I dropped out! And while the saying is that *"quitters never win and winners never quit,"* most of my "wins" came after I stopped the struggling and striving. I'm neither proud nor ashamed to admit that I've quit a lot in my life.

Now, this is <u>not</u> a lesson to encourage quitting. This is merely to illustrate the glory of God, because any success I currently have has come from surrendering to the Grace of God and then following whatever Guidance has come after my surrender. God's strength is often made perfect in my personal weakness. And my life is a testimony to spiritual paradox. I call it Opposite World.

Whenever I have tried to make money, I ended up in debt. Anytime I tried to date or be in a relationship, the men ran from me like I was a rabid dog. When I tried to get people to come to my classes, I would be standing in an empty meeting room with no students. When I've tried to get healthy, my body falls apart and I gain weight daily. So, I stopped struggling. I gave up and gave my life to Spirit and said, *"I'm a mess, but if You can make good use of me, go for it."* And that is when my joy and true success began and my mess became my message. We all have our unique path to success and we must honor it if we want to be happy.

AFFIRMATION 25

I FOCUS ON SAVORING AND ENJOYING THE PRESENT.

"My present happiness is all I see." -ACIM

SOMETIMES THE PROBLEM with positive thinking, abundance principles, spiritual healing teachings and such is that rather than simply expanding our vision beyond old limited thinking, people can start to feel ungrateful and dissatisfied with their present good.

Rather than simply visioning an expanding future of greater good, people can start to look around at their present life and instead of blessing it in order to increase the good, they start focusing on what has become threadbare, or how their mate lacks this or that, or how their own body is starting to wrinkle or sag, or that their job is not their "dream" career. In other words, the ego mind has co-opted spiritual teachings as a way to steal our present joy. The ego is all about arriving somewhere different. Spirit is all about enjoying each step of the journey. DO NOT LET NEGATIVITY AND FEAR STEAL YOUR JOY!

As we bless our present moment – even the shabby rug and "imperfect" mate, we are setting the right vibration not only for our future good, but for a present that we feel grateful for because we have learned how to take our own emotional journey. We are not waiting for the world or situations to make us happy. We DECIDE to be happy by guiding our own thoughts in the here and now.

I am savoring and enjoying my now through the practice of gratitude and appreciation. I bless everything in my world.

AFFIRMATION 26

EVERYONE WINS IN MY SPACE, INCLUDING ME.

"Because God's equal children have everything they cannot compete." - ACIM

IN SPIRIT THERE IS NO COMPETITION - there is plenty of good to go around. We do not have to sacrifice our own joy so that others around us can thrive. Nor do we need to win at the expense of others.

Each one of us has a vibratory atmosphere that we carry with us through the world each day. It is created by our thoughts, moods, beliefs and attitudes. As we change our thinking, we change our vibratory atmosphere. And since like attracts like, we will tend to attract others who would be good partners for our particular vibratory atmosphere.

If we believe we are worthless garbage, we will attract those who will treat us that way. If we believe that Life loves us and that only good lies before us, we will attract others who will reflect that back to us. We are setting the tone of our day either consciously on unconsciously – and we then co-create with those around us a day that reflects that tone.

I am free to choose the tone I want to set in my life each day and I release all others to do the same. It is wonderful that we all get to choose and I am happy to take responsibility for choosing what works for me.

AFFIRMATION 27

I AM NOT HERE TO FIX OR SAVE ANYONE.

"To teach is to demonstrate." -ACIM

HOW WONDERFUL IT IS when we are able to make a positive difference in the lives of others. How depressing, hopeless and stressful it is to take responsibility for others. For myself, I realized many years ago that I was not really able to save anyone but myself. After spending years of wasted energy on trying to fix or save others, I realized that I was mostly just driving us all crazy with my good ideas and inspiring wisdom. Ultimately, people do what they want to do. So, I came to find that all my preaching, recommending and pearls of wisdom were just making me more separate from others instead of closer.

I had to give up being savior and save myself. I was the one who wanted and needed my pearls of wisdom and inspirational talks. I was the one who needed my wisdom and recommendations. It wasn't that they wouldn't listen to me – it's that *I* wouldn't listen to me. I needed to stay in my own yard, in my own business. I had to release my hostages.

Much of my life now is about helping people help themselves by simply sharing my own experience and the spiritual tools that I use. I cannot teach peace and happiness unless I am peaceful and happy myself. We teach best through demonstration and modeling behaviors, rather than through preaching and lecturing.

I am not here to fix or save anyone but myself. And as I accept healing for myself, others can be healed as I demonstrate how simple it really is.

Affirmation 28

I Am Willing to Change.

*"The changes the ego seeks to make
are not really changes."* -ACIM

THERE IS A NEW THOUGHT MOTTO that goes, *"Change your thinking, change your life."* But we are taught to think the other way around – that if we just change some aspect of our lives, then we will think and feel differently.

So, though it may seem contradictory, I've found that what has been truly helpful to increasing my joy and peace is this statement: *"I am perfect just as I am, and I am willing to change."* These two things actually go together quite well. We tend to think that the only reason for us to change is because there is something wrong with us. This is not so. Change is a natural part of life. What really hurts us is resistance to change.

I can accept myself exactly as I am – even celebrating myself just as I am, and still be willing to change. My essential Self is perfect, but my behavior is not. And as I continue to spiritually mature, I naturally change, not through self-will and forcing but through an increasing awareness and wisdom of what works and what doesn't work. As we allow healing to take place, certain things that no longer serve will begin to naturally drop from us. We become less and less attracted to what hurts or inhibits us and others.

I love and approve of myself just as I am, and I am willing to change.

AFFIRMATION 29

THE BETTER IT GETS, THE BETTER IT GETS.

*"Be lifted up, and from a higher place look down upon it.
From there will your perspective be quite different."* -ACIM

INERTIA IS THE TENDENCY OF THE OBJECT to go in whatever direction it's been going in. An object at rest tends to stay at rest and an object in motion tends to stay in motion. And everything will keep on just as it is unless we choose a new direction by setting a new vision.

"The rich get richer and the poor get poorer. When it rains is pours. The better it gets, the better it gets. The worse it gets, the worse it gets." These are all energy patterns. EVERYTHING in the Universe is energy. We are energy. Life is energy itself.

In the various areas of our lives, the way things are going is the way they will continue to go unless we make a change. If we like the way things are going in a particular area, then our part is to relax into that energy pattern and keep on affirming that we like where this is going.

If we do not like the direction in some area of our lives, then rather than opposing we must shift our vision. We do not fight against or go into battle with the problem – we rise above the battleground entirely. We cannot solve problems from the same level of Consciousness as the problem. Instead, we go directly to God and the problems dissolve as we begin to give our energy to the new direction.

I rest in God today as I give my attention to what is good in my world. Life loves me and there is nothing to fear.

AFFIRMATION 30

LIFE IS RESPONDING TO ME.

"What kind of day will you decide to have?" - ACIM

THERE IS A DYNAMIC SOMETHING in the Universe that is responding to our thoughts, words, attitudes and actions. Life is not happening to us – Life is responding to us. Therefore, let us consciously and deliberately use this Something in positive ways by choosing the thoughts that we would like to see manifest in our lives today.

We are not deciding what will happen today, we are deciding what energies we want to activate and channel. If we merely react to whatever is happening around us, we are living in a victim mentality and we are at the effect of everything outside of us. The real Power is not out there – it's inside of us, but if we do not deliberately activate the energies that we want to dominate our day, then we will live by default instead of with deliberate intention.

What are the energies you want to activate within yourself today? What do you want to feel? What are the thoughts you want to dominate your mind? Make these your dominant intention as you partner with the dynamic Something to work out all the details of the how.

I guide my mind and set my deliberate intentions for the day. It's not my job to make things happen, but merely to line up behind my own intentions and then allow the Universe to lead the way as I keep showing up for my greater good.

AFFIRMATION 31

I VIGILANTLY MAINTAIN MY PEACE & JOY TODAY.

"Your vigilance is the sign that you want Him to guide you. Vigilance does require effort, but only until you learn that effort itself is not necessary." -ACIM

ALL THE EGO WANTS TO DO IS steal our joy in this moment. The ego thought system isn't about ruining our lives - it's about ruining THIS moment by focusing us away from joy and peace, toward whatever is even mildly disturbing. Just one person blowing their horn at us in traffic can be enough to steal away our joy IF WE ALLOW IT.

The ego thought system is extremely vigilant about focusing on guilt – in others and in us. And that means we must be just as vigilant for our peace and joy. Ultimately it's not so much that our joy is stolen, as it is that we throw it away. That person blows the horn and we use that as the justification for mentally attacking them and defending ourselves. In that very moment, WE have thrown our peace and joy out the window and are focusing on the guilt and attack.

Big deal, so what? The point is to get right back on the highlighted route as soon as you possibly can by remembering to be vigilant for your peace and joy instead of being vigilant about things that disturb you.

No one and nothing can take away my peace and joy today. I am breathing in the peace of God and my heart is full of joy and love.

AFFIRMATION 32

I WILL NOT ARGUE FOR MY LIMITATIONS.

"Let me not see myself as limited." -ACIM

YOU ARE PROBABLY FAMILIAR WITH the quote, *"Argue for your limitations, and sure enough their yours."* This needs to include the limitations we perceive in our family, our environment, the culture, the company, the economy, and the limitations of the people around us. In general, let's not argue for limitation because with God, ALL things are possible.

So often, we don't even realize that we are arguing for limitations. We think we are just stating the "facts." As if Infinite Intelligence could be held back by "facts." Often the facts are just a stressful story that we have failed to question.

The actress and writer Ruth Gordon used to say, *"Never face the facts."* She meant don't let the facts deter you from doing what you are called to do. She knew the "facts" were stacked against her in terms of her making a living as an actress, but she chose to not let that inhibit her from moving forward. In fact, she moved so far forward that she won an Academy Award. The "facts" were nothing but a limiting story. "Incurable" is not a fact – it's just a story of the past. Maybe "it" hasn't ever been cured yet, but that has nothing to do with a Child of God.

I choose to believe that nothing can stop my good from coming through in perfect timing and in perfect ways as I keep on showing up, prepared, on time, doing what I said I would do, with a good attitude.

AFFIRMATION 33

I AM CONSULTING A HIGHER AUTHORITY.

"If you are trusting in your own strength, you have every reason to be apprehensive, anxious and fearful." - ACIM

YEARS AGO I TOOK A GROUP OF FRIENDS to the Arlington Theater in Santa Barbara to hear Maya Angelou speak. It was a magical and inspiring evening that I will never forget – particularly since I've quoted her in my talks so frequently.

Of course my favorite inspirational story of hers is when her son nearly lost his life in an accident, and when she rushed to the hospital to be by his side, the doctor gave her a horrible prognosis. She was told that he might die, or at the very least would never walk again, to which she very sternly replied, *"What do you know? I've consulted a Higher Authority!"* Wow, that is power – that is faith!

She didn't take her son out of the hospital or remove him from the doctor's care. She wasn't chastising the doctor about his medical skills. She was reminding him that none of us is God or have any idea what is actually possible when it comes to healing. But, there is a Power and a Presence within us that does know and that CAN do what up until now has been impossible.

I will not let the voices of fear guide my life today. I am consulting a Higher Authority in all that I undertake to do, be, or have. What has not been possible for me before is easy for the Power of God within me. I am leaning not on my own understanding, but am entrusting myself to the Highest of the High.

Affirmation 34

I Think About What I'm Thinking About.

"It is much more helpful to remind you that you do not guard your thoughts carefully enough." - ACIM

We hear a lot about "mindfulness" in various spiritual circles. It's really just another way of saying "pay attention." In today's lesson, we are being mindful of our mind – being mindful of what we are thinking. I tell people, *"think about what you are thinking about"* rather than just mindlessly ruminating. Be AWARE of what your mind is doing.

A Course in Miracles tells us *"an untrained mind can accomplish nothing."* What this really means is that an untrained mind can accomplish nothing good. An untrained mind CAN accomplish a lot of stress, panic, anxiety, attack, chaos and so on. But that's not really our goal. In fact, this untrained mind HAS been trained – in the exact wrong way. What we want instead is a mind that is spacious, open, happy and connected to Infinite Wisdom.

We begin by paying attention to our thoughts and noticing more quickly when we are taking the mental detour into fear. Take a moment now to reflect on the nature of your recent thoughts. What has been your mental state? What have you been mentally chewing on? It's not so much what you are thinking as HOW you are thinking about it. To keep it simple, there are two thought systems, one feels good and one feels bad. Choose the good feeling one more.

I am becoming mindful of the difference between thoughts that feel good, and the ones that don't. I now <u>choose</u> my thoughts as I place a guard at the door of my mind to keep.

AFFIRMATION 35

I WORK FOR GOD, NOT FOR PEOPLE OR MONEY AND YET
MONEY FLOWS TO ME IN EVER-INCREASING AMOUNTS.

"God is my source." - ACIM

WE ARE ALL ON A HUGE TEMP ASSIGNMENT here on Planet
Earth. None of us will be staying on past the end of our
assignment. Nothing here belongs to us – not land, or
houses, or people or even the body we inhabit. Everything is
on loan from Corporate Headquarters and will be returned at
the end of this gig. Ashes to ashes, and dust to dust. It's all
traded in until we receive all that is needed for our next
Cosmic Assignment.

I often tell my students that I am the semi-retired
executive secretary to Jesus, here to run His errands at the
WeHo Zendo Joy Academy. This delights and amuses me
more than I can say, but I also actually believe it. It's my
daily experience. And because of this belief and experience,
I have gradually changed from a very anxious tense ego-
driven fearful extremely ATTACHED person into a much
more peaceful, relaxed, humbled joyful temp-worker
traveling on this glorious planet through time and space.

Basically, we are all working for God, not for people or
for companies. The people or companies are just the
particular TEMPORARY avenue through which we are
channeled money, opportunities, perks, benefits and so on.

*I work for God as part of this Universal Cosmic Corporation
for the Advancement of Souls. I am very well paid and
compensated for I work for the best Boss and the most
successful Company in the Universe.*

AFFIRMATION 36

I CAN CHOOSE THE RIGHT DIRECTION FOR MYSELF.

*"A journey of a thousand miles
begins with a single step."* – LAO TZU

THE LIFE OF SPIRITUAL CONSCIOUSNESS is not a race to a final destination. There is no competition and no place to arrive at beyond the here and now. In fact, the future is only a man-made concept that has nothing to do with reality.

How much forward progress we think we've made in any day, week, or month is less important than that we are simply going in the right direction. Many people are speedily going in the wrong direction and won't realize it for quite some time because they are too busy trying to make good time to realize their happiness is shrinking as they go.

So what is the "right" direction when it comes to a Spiritual Consciousness? Inner peace and joy. And we can tell we are going in the right direction by how much inner peace and joy we have today, in this very moment. In this sense, we are arriving every moment – we have not delayed our lives until later. We are thinking in terms of progress, not perfection.

As I guide my mind to the thoughts that increase my joy and inner peace, I can feel when I am going in the right direction and make correction as I go. There is no hurry. I am savoring and enjoying the journey.

AFFIRMATION 37

I AM ALLOWING MORE GOOD INTO MY WORLD.

*"The roses under my window make no reference to former
roses or better ones; they are what they are; they exist with
God today. There is no time to them. There is simply the
rose; it is perfect in every moment of its existence."*
— RALPH WALDO EMERSON

OUR SPIRITUAL TASK is to allow ourselves to be gently
opened like a flower in the sunlight. Our Spiritual
Maturation process can be as orderly as any other part of
nature. The reason it often isn't is only because of our
resistance and our determination to control the process. We
are trying to rush our good, or to resist what we fear. This
perverts the natural process of our growth.

Our Spiritual Growth then is not about becoming
something other than what we are, but of relaxing into a
natural process of blossoming into MORE of our authentic
selves. It's not just that we cannot compare ourselves to the
person next to us – it is an act of violence to the Soul to
compare yourself to your younger self, or to your idealized
fantasy self.

The life of joy and inner peace that we desire is not a
matter of achievement and acquisition – it is a life of
gradually becoming more and more oceanic in our capacity
to channel more Life through us.

*Each day I am allowing more Life to flow through me. I am
a Divine Channel of Infinite Love and my capacity to accept
more good is increasing with ease and joy all the time.*

AFFIRMATION 38

I AM CALMLY PRESENT AND PAYING ATTENTION.

"You are much too tolerant of mind wandering . . ." – ACIM

THE VAST MAJORITY OF OUR LESSONS IN LIFE are simply to "pay attention." As someone who is well into my third decade of teaching I cannot tell you how often a student is asking me a question about something that is answered on the sheet of paper they are holding in their hands, or is stated 6 times in the email they are responding to, or is answered in the paragraph just above the one they are asking about. But we have a difficult time focusing on just one thing – our minds are often extremely busy, even frantic.

All of this mental rushing around actually interferes with making good progress because of all the messes it creates that need to be cleaned up later. This is no reason to feel guilty or get down on ourselves – it's merely a gentle wakeup call to FOCUS on what is happening right now – to pay attention and *be here now*. Taking our time saves time, and even lives.

It's okay to take my time. I am patient with myself and others as I allow myself to do one thing at a time. I am fully present and open to see and experience what is happening in my present moment. All is well.

AFFIRMATION 39

I SEE MYSELF IN EVERYONE TODAY.

"The Holy Spirit teaches you that if you look only at yourself you cannot find yourself, because that is not what you are."
— ACIM

AS SOCIAL BEINGS we tend to be obsessed with being seen. Whether we want to be famous and have the whole world see us, or we want to be seen intimately by one person, there is that yearning within us to be seen, heard, known – and often seen a certain way. One of the things that gets ego very activated is feeling invisible to others.

We have a choice at moments like this   we can become desperate and start doing things to get attention, or we can use this as a transformative experience to realize that the self that wants attention is not the true Self at all. We can stop trying to get anyone to give us attention and instead begin to focus on discovering and remembering who we are beyond the ego's body-identification. Instead of thinking we are this creature we see in the mirror or in the mirror of the eyes of another, we can go deeper.

This is the big shift, when we become less interested in others getting to know us, and become interested in getting to know them. As we begin to see and praise those around us, we begin to activate that same vibration within ourselves. As we focus on their magnificence, it activates that same feeling of magnificence in ourselves.

I release any need for attention and approval and remember Who I am.

AFFIRMATION 40

I STAY HAPPILY IN MY OWN YARD TODAY.

"I can find only three kinds of business in the universe: mine, yours, and God's (For me, the word God means "reality." Reality is God, because it rules. Anything that's out of my control, your control, and everyone else's control – I call that God's business.) " – BYRON KATIE

THE PERSONAL MANTRA that I teach our Urban Mystics most often in regards to succeeding in life is this: show up, prepared, on time, doing what you said you would do, with a good attitude. Everything else is out of our control.

Yes, we have an influence on others and on the world around us, but not control. Trying to control our mate, children, neighbors, parents, co-workers, employees, and the world is usually frustrating and depressing.

When we decide to stay in our own business, or as I say, in our own yard, it doesn't mean that we retreat from the world and stop interacting with people. Instead, I say we are freeing the hostages we've taken when we are mentally holding them captive to all of our ideas about what they should or shouldn't be doing. Instead, we work on cleaning up our own yard and enjoying the fruits of our labor.

I am happily enjoying working in my own garden today and I joyfully release all others to their highest and best good. I have no idea what is best for others or what anyone else should be doing. Today I choose the peace of God right here in my own yard.

AFFIRMATION 41

THIS IS A DAY OF HOLY ENCOUNTERS

*"Ideally, psychotherapy is a series of holy encounters
in which brothers meet to bless each other and to
receive the peace of God."* – ACIM

THE PURPOSE OF ALL RELATIONSHIPS is that they become holy. Yet, in so many ways we tend to think in terms of getting something, fixing something, changing something, or someone.

While the quote above references psychotherapy, the purpose of ALL relationships is for us to bless each other and receive the peace of God from our joining together, regardless of how fleeting or seemingly "meaningless" the encounter. Quite often what is actually meaningless is the reason we *think* we are there – even if we are arrogant enough to think that we are there to help heal someone. It's so much bigger and yet simpler than that.

How simple, profound and beautiful today can be if this thought is remembered periodically as you go about your day interacting with the world around you. Try today not to miss an opportunity to meet this goal of blessing all you meet as you receive the peace of God from the encounter.

No matter where I go or what I do today, my goal is to bless all those I see or think of, and to open up to receive the limitless bountiful peace of God.

AFFIRMATION 42

I RELEASE THE NEED TO CONTROL LIFE.

*"You who cannot even control yourself
should hardly aspire to control the Universe.* – ACIM

GIVING UP CONTROL is actually giving up something that we don't really have to begin with when it comes to anything outside of us. People do what they want to do, and life goes the way it's going to go. What we are really surrendering is the *illusion* of control.

What we exchange control for is non-attached influence. We have a tremendous influential force through our words, intentions, actions, attitudes, and thoughts. Giving up control is not throwing our hands up and walking away in frustration in this kind of scenario. Instead, we center and ground ourselves within, knowing that the Universe is always responding to our vibration. We are not trying to make anything work – we are relaxing our resistance in order to LET things work.

When we focus on simply being a positive influence instead of a dictator, we are allowing Greater Forces to begin to move into the situation as we work on releasing our tension and fears.

Let go. Breathe. Relax. Center yourself in the peace and love of God and trust that whatever you need to know will be revealed to you in perfect timing and ways.

I trust the Universe to guide me and all the people and situations in my life in ways that work for us all. I allow myself to let go and let God.

AFFIRMATION 43

I BLESS MY CURRENT CIRCUMSTANCES.

"I bless the world because I bless myself." – ACIM

MANY OF US HAVE A TENDENCY OF RESISTING anything that we do not like in our lives. But because of how Consciousness works, what we resist, we are focusing on – and what we focus on with resistance gets locked into place. The more we resist, the more it persists.

When we choose to bless every aspect of our lives, even that which we do not like or approve of, we've made friends with the circumstances of our lives and we have made a little crack for peace to enter through.

Acceptance and approval are not the same thing. We can accept something without approving of it. We tend to be afraid that if we accept things as they are, they will never change or get better. But usually the opposite is truer. When we make friends with the circumstances of our lives – even making friends with a disease in our body, we are not saying that we want or approve of it, but only that we do not want to destroy our peace by waging war with anyone or anything. We want the peace of God instead.

And once we've established internal peace, it is much easier to make positive changes through self-love and clarity, instead of through fighting and resistance.

I bless my world with love and gratitude today as I let go of all resistance and focus anything that brings more joy to my heart.

AFFIRMATION 44

I AM LED AND GUIDED BY GRACE TODAY.

"God's Voice speaks to me all through the day." – ACIM

WE ARE NOT ALONE, cast adrift in a world of chaos and confusion. We have Help, and help that *knows* rather than guesses. But this Help is not imposed upon us. We have free will, which means the freedom to think and believe whatever we choose. Even if we are locked up in a cell or living in a body that does not work or respond in the way we want it to, we can still take the journey of deliberate thought. Our bodies can be in complete bondage, but we still have the freedom to choose our own thoughts.

When we choose to be led and guided by the Voice for God within us, we are simply tuning our receiver to the frequency of love, joy, peace and Infinite wisdom instead of going it alone with all the static of the frequencies of fear and chaos.

The God Station never stops broadcasting. It plays all day and all night long without ceasing. It is the voice of kindness and serenity within us and it is available whenever we tune take even one moment to make the connection and LISTEN.

"Beloved Divine Spirit, I assume You are in control here. Let me know if there is anything I need to know. I'm available and listening."

AFFIRMATION 45

MY VALVE IS OPEN WIDE TODAY AND
THE LOVE IS FREELY FLOWING IN AND OUT.

*"True prayer must avoid the pitfall of asking to entreat.
Ask, rather, to receive what is already given;
to accept what is already there."* – ACIM

LOVE IS ALL AROUND AND FULLY AVAILABLE to those with eyes to see and ears to hear. But the Course teaches us that we are not really afraid of fearful things – we are afraid of love. We are afraid of love even as we yearn for it and desperately seek it out. Love terrifies the ego thought system, which is built on the belief in specialness and separation.

This ego thought system tells us that we need a certain kind or form of love – that we need our loved ones to behave in a certain way, or to agree with us, or to "have our back" in a dangerous world. We want our children or parents to shape up in some way, or we want approval, or to be truly seen in a certain way. These are ways of blocking love by invalidating it when it is right in front of us. In this sense, love is a taking of hostages who we keep in the prison of our minds, trying to manipulate them into being different than they are.

But love is so much simpler than this. Love is about RELEASING rather than holding tight. Love is the gentle acceptance of what has been given instead of judgment about how it's still not quite perfect.

My world is full of love and lit by miracles. I release myself and all others from harsh and critical expectations as I soften and open my heart to all the love that is flowing.

AFFIRMATION 46

I ASK AND IT IS GIVEN.

"You cannot answer a question that hasn't been asked."
— ESTHER HICKS

FROM TIME TO TIME, I will have my groups repeat after me this mantra – *"No one wants my good advice!"* And it's as true of me as anyone else- even though people have actually given money in order to sit there and supposedly hear my good advice. Mostly what people really want is love.

But somehow we get all confused when we see people struggling or in pain, and we project our story onto them of how we would feel in their place, or we make a lot of assumptions about what they are doing wrong or what they should do. This is the opposite of helpful in most cases.

And though our motives and intentions may be quite good, our advice is usually ineffective if the person has not specifically ASKED us for that kind of help. It's said that we have one mouth and two ears and should use them accordingly. To listen at least twice as much as we speak is a good guideline most of the time.

I am not here to fix or correct anyone. I listen deeply and then speak from the Guidance within me & I release everyone to their own highest good.

Affirmation 47

I AM AUTHENTICALLY MYSELF & IT FEELS WONDERFUL.

"Again there are many who are living far below their possibilities because they are continually handing over their individualities to others. Do you want to be a power in the world? Then be yourself." – RALPH WALDO TRINE

EACH OF US IS A UNIQUE EXPRESSION of the One Life manifested in form. There is no one to compare yourself to in any way. No one can replace you in this glorious Multiverse nor do just what you came here to do or be. There is no comparison to glorious magnificent you.

The saying goes, *"Be yourself. Everyone else is taken."* Others can inspire us – and we may even take on some of the characteristics and style of those we admire, but this is only helpful to us if it resonates with our own inner being and is not done as a way to try to water down our authenticity because we've judged ourselves as lacking. Originality just for the sake of originality is no better than outright copying if it's not coming from something within us that wants to be expressed.

Purple is not "better" than beige – it's just different. Different is not better than sameness. Whatever you are, be that as fully and honestly as possible and let that be the magnetic force that draws your right life to you.

I love and approve of myself just as I am, and just as I am not. I am happy to be exactly who and what I am today.

AFFIRMATION 48

I MAKE PEACE WITH WHERE I AM.

"Let all things be exactly as they are." – ACIM

GOING TO WAR WITH THE CIRUCUMSTANCES of our lives and the state of our bodies and affairs can be such a frustrating and depressing waste of time and energy. A Course in Miracles teaches that we have an "authorship" problem. We think we made ourselves and so we think we can fix or change ourselves. We see ourselves as projects to work on.

The spiritual premise is that we are created by God and if we need changing, only God can truly change us – if we will allow it and not fight the change. It is yet another spiritual paradox that the most profound changes come first from a place of acceptance rather than of resistance.

This kind of acceptance does not mean that we approve of or like what is – but it does mean that we've given up waging war against anyone or anything. We want the peace of God instead. Even a recovering alcoholic can tell you that until she accepts that she has a drinking problem, she can never become sober. Acceptance is the first step to deep and lasting change, if change is necessary. We can make peace with where we are, even while we are working to create positive change.

I make peace with who I am and with my life exactly as it is today.

AFFIRMATION 49

THAT'S FOR ME!

*"Beware of the temptation to
perceive yourself unfairly treated."* – ACIM

WE CAN LOOK AT THE GOOD THAT SOMEONE ELSE has or does that we would like to experience and we can either be jealous and depressed, or we can be inspired and uplifted. We can look around at our current circumstances and feel deprived and like a failure, or we can align ourselves with the greater good that we see others living and say, *"That's for me too!"*

It's not up to us to decide if others deserve the good that they are experiencing in their lives. That's between them and their God. It's up to us to take our OWN emotional journey and to get busy aligning ourselves with our own greater good.

I give myself the gift of celebrating another day on the planet by aligning myself with the bountiful good of my Father's Kingdom.

Affirmation 50

I Ask for and Receive the Help I Need Today.

*"You are not bereft of help,
and Help that knows the answer."* – ACIM

PERHAPS THE MOST SIMPLE AND PROFOUND PRAYER that we can ever utter is *"God, Help me."* The issue for many of us is that we find it difficult to ask for help. And if we find it difficult to ask for help, then much of the time we may not even remember that it is an option. Of course it is the most powerful and effective option of all.

William Thetford, who was the co-scribe of A Course in Miracles, was somewhat famous for asking for Help all day long. His roommates would sometimes hear him alone in his room saying aloud, *"Help me do this!"* What a simple, childlike and miraculous way to live and go through life.

The fact is, the Course tells us that we do not ask for too much but for far too little. It's not possible to bug the Holy Spirit too much when we are asking for real daily Help in all that we undertake.

Divine Spirit, I need Your Help today in all things. I seek Your Presence and Your guidance as I give my hands, feet and voice to You to joyfully direct and use.

AFFIRMATION 51

RESENTMENTS AND GRIEVANCES HAVE NO PLACE IN ME.

"I will forgive and this will disappear." – ACIM

IT WOULD BE SO MUCH EASIER to love people if they would just behave themselves and act more lovably, wouldn't it? Yet we are surrounded by people who pretty much do what they choose rather than following our prescribed plan for what is proper and improper behavior for human beings sharing the planet with us. How frustrating!

Therefore if we truly want the peace that passes all understanding, we cannot afford to carry any grievances or resentments on our backs. Peace and resentment don't go together.

Our goal is to travel lightly through the world. This means being aware of when we are starting to have attack thoughts about anyone or anything, including ourselves. The faster we notice the first attack thought, the easier to not start building a case file of evidence about anything. We can drop the case right there and surrender it to the Higher Court to handle. Our job is not to be a lawyer for the prosecution, but rather to be a witness to miracles. We can do one or the other, but not both. The vision of one world costs us the vision of the other.

True forgiveness is not about going over all the evidence endlessly. It's about handing over all the files to the Holy Spirit to sort out while we go about the business of choosing peace.

Today I give up being a prosecutor & become a peacemaker.

AFFIRMATION 52

I LINE UP WITH MY GREATER GOOD.

"Miracles are examples of right thinking, aligning your perceptions with truth as God created it." – ACIM

GET IN AGREEMENT WITH YOUR INTENTIONS TODAY. Get in agreement with God's Truth. Sometimes people make the good move of surrendering control to Spirit, but then start to act as if they are now victims to some will outside of them which takes away all personal individual responsibility and choice. This is ego black-or-white thinking. We are in partnership with the Divine, not puppets dancing on strings.

We have a very important part of the co-creative process, and that is to line up with our own intentions rather than falling into doubt or even hope. Hope is for those who have no faith or who do not understand how Law operates.

Our part is to set our intentions with NON-ATTACHMENT to the outcome and then to affirm, expect, and exercise our faith in happy outcomes and happy journeys. Master Jesus would give thanks BEFORE the manifestations of good in order to ACTIVATE faith consciousness. Gratitude is a way to dissolve doubt. Remember, we don't have faith in a specific outcome; we have faith that God is on the field and that we are held perfectly in His hands. We affirm that things are already working and that only good lies before us.

Things are lining up for me now and I am in agreement with God's Law of Infinite Good. I am aligned with Source.

AFFIRMATION 53

MONEY LOVES ME AND I OPEN TO RECEIVE IT NOW.

"Prosperity is your divine right." – REV. TERRY

THERE IS SO MUCH MONEY OUT THERE in the world just looking for a place to land. There is no lack of money, no lack of opportunities. There is only a lack of understanding and receptivity.

Our work is not to figure out ways to "get" more money but rather of how to expand our consciousness to a greater mental equivalency - a vibrational-matching and receptivity to money.

Like everything else, money is energy. And energy flows to where there is an opening to receive it. This is a very Taoist principle in which Lao Tzu taught that the Tao is like water, it flows downward by gravity and fills the open spaces.

Money cannot flow into a tense constricted mind. If we are judging money or people who have it, we have closed our hearts to money and it will simply flow elsewhere. Money is as neutral as a rock on the ground. A rock can be used as the cornerstone to a magnificent home filled with love or it can be used as a weapon to break a window.

Learn to welcome money by giving it a place in your consciousness that is open and welcoming. Speak joyfully and kindly about money and it will begin to be drawn to you. Money can be great fun.

Money loves me & is drawn to me like static cling. I always have more than enough to share & to spare. Money is a fun friend to play with in creative joyful ways.

AFFIRMATION 54

I AM HERE TO LET MY CORK FLOAT.

"Light and joy and peace abide in me." – ACIM

IMAGINE THAT YOUR JOY is like the cork from a bottle bobbing up and down on the surface of the ocean. Our task each day is to guide our mind in such a way that the cork keeps on bobbing and floating.

Fear and negativity are like sinkers tied to the cork, which keeps dragging it down below the surface of the water, trying to steal away our joy. Then, it seems like that sinking is caused by the circumstances that we face each day. But in reality, it's the story we tell ourselves about those circumstances that cause that sinking feeling.

This is why the most important journey that we take each day is our emotional journey. The emotional journey is the story we tell ourselves, the attitude we have about our life.

What makes your cork float? What brings you joy? Think about that today and let it kick-start your emotional journey every day. Each morning I make a list titled, "What I Love" and I write down 5 to 10 things that I love and that activate my joy. Most of them are extremely simple – things like, pens and paper, a cup of coffee, my soft bed, gorgeous blue sky mornings, the heat of Palm Springs, good friends, and so on.

C'mon. Join us in the League of Corkfloaters!

I am letting my cork float today as I take my emotional journey of joy and peace. I am grateful and full of love as I notice all the good in my world.

AFFIRMATION 55

I AM IMAGINING MY WAY TO HEAVEN TODAY.

"Imagination is the first faculty, and takes precedence over all the other powers or elements of consciousness."
— JOSEPH MURPHY

IMAGINE. WHAT A WONDERFUL WORD. Many people don't realize what a vast amount of time is spent in imagining since we tend to think of imagining as something that children at play do – or that perhaps it is only the domain of artists, or even lazy folks who *"dream their lives away."*

But we cannot help imagining. We are creators, made by a Creator as an extension of Itself. Therefore, imagination is a primary aspect of our Consciousness and cannot be stopped. Worrying is nothing more than misuse of the creative faculty by imagining catastrophe. And I'm sure you've probably worried plenty in your lifetime.

One of our wonderful Practitioners uses his imagination regularly by writing me an actual letter, either weekly or monthly - but he does not send the letter. It's for his own imaginative use. In the letter he writes me what is basically a post-dated letter from a month, or 6 months, or 1 year in the future. And in the letter he writes to me of all the wonderful things that he has experienced and accomplished and how great it all feels. He doesn't know HOW it all happened, just that it did. THAT is creative imagination at its best! Try it and see for yourself. He literally went from a temp job to tenured professor in just a few short years of this process.

I have a wonderful imagination and I use it positively, purposely and joyfully today to fill my world with good!

AFFIRMATION 56

I AM SAFE - IT'S ONLY CHANGE.

"I am at home. Fear is the stranger here." – ACIM

THE BUDDHA TAUGHT THAT WE SUFFER because we seek for permanence and stability in that which is by its very nature ever changing.

In fact, change is the one thing that we can count on in life. Learning to weather the storms and to enjoy the sunny days when they are here is a huge part of our spiritual practice and growth. There is something to be mined from each experience as it comes and we waste our precious energy and time when we resist what is happening right now. The more adaptable we are, the more we can thrive under any and all circumstances.

When everything outside of us is changing in ways that make us uncomfortable, it is even more delicious than ever to go within to cultivate a deepening relationship with what is changeless and eternal. These are the times when the rubber meets the road and we get to see what we truly believe and to decide what we are going to focus on. Do not let the ego steal your peace. Relax any resistance and focus again on how you want to FEEL, regardless of what is going on in your outer world today. This is how we set the internal GPS back to Center.

I can have peace even in the midst of change. I see change as positive growth and an expansion of my own Consciousness, preparing me for even more good. I am curious to see how God works all of this out for my good.

AFFIRMATION 57

MY HEART IS OPEN.

"The course does not aim at teaching the meaning of love,
for that is beyond what can be taught.
It does aim, however, at removing the blocks to the
awareness of love's presence, which is
your natural inheritance."– ACIM

THERE IS A STORY I HEARD a famous actress tell of meeting the love of her life after a very public and messy divorce from her also-famous first husband.

On one of her first dates with this new man, after all the pain, public embarrassment and heartbreak, they sat on a bench overlooking the ocean and, knowing about her divorce and perhaps testing the waters, he quietly and plainly asked her, *"So, how's your heart?"* And without a moment's hesitation she replied, *"open."*

That's the miracle of love and the magic of a heart that is willing to let go of the old story of the past. They went on to marry and have children and started a whole new story together because of the willingness to release the blocks to the awareness of love knocking on the door. And this is our choice each moment, every day, in thousands of little and not so little ways. Will we grow harder and more closed, or softer and more open? There is no order of difficulty in miracles.

I open my heart to love today instead of guarding myself. I let go of defensiveness and resistance in order to let my heart be free to give and receive the love that heals us all.

AFFIRMATION 58

LOVE FILLS MY HEART AND MY WORLD.

"Your gratitude to your brother is the only gift I want . . .
Love does not conquer all things,
but it does set all things right." – ACIM

ERNEST HOLMES, WHO WAS THE FOUNDER of the Centers for Spiritual Living, spent most of his life teaching the mental laws of New Thought. But he was also very clear that we should not let ourselves get so wrapped up in the *"law of attraction"* that our prayers and affirmations become cold and mechanical, used in an attempt to *"get rich quick"* or even to heal a sick body. In fact, near the end of his life he told someone that he wished he'd spent more time talking about the love principle.

But, it's hard to talk about love in a way that isn't merely sentimental and manipulative – and it can't be taught in a class or a book. It can only be cultivated through shifts in our perception, in our ways of seeing the world. Jesus was a master at love, so for many of us He is the great example, but he is only one of the many faces that the teachers of love take.

A Course in Miracles encourages us to be teachers of love by demonstrating it – and gratitude activates and demonstrates the love vibration. As the Course says, *"for love cannot be far behind a grateful heart and a thankful mind."*

I express my love today through words of gratitude and praise. I tell people what I appreciate about them and I lift their spirit with my sincere words.

AFFIRMATION 59

I CAN EASILY GET BACK ON TRACK WHEN I FALTER.

"Retrogression is temporary." – ACIM

WE CAN TURN A DOWNWARD SPIRAL into an upward spiral if we are willing to let go of whatever story or resistance we are holding onto – and it does not have to take long at all.

Once we've admitted how we currently feel (instead of trying to push it down, pretend it isn't there, or operate over it) we can then take a deep breath and release all those thoughts and feelings back to the nothingness from whence they came. Let them dissolve into the white Light of the Holy Spirit's love as you let go of blame, guilt and shame. Then, CHOOSE ONCE AGAIN.

This means, decide how you WANT to feel now. Don't try to figure out HOW you will get there – for now, your part is simply setting the internal GPS system for the destination and then following the highlighted route by reaching for any little thought that feels even a little bit better.

I don't have to figure all of this out right now or know exactly what to do. I simply want to have the peace and joy of God back in my awareness and so I release all attack thoughts against myself and others as I return to the path of Light. My Guide is here with me now and my only concern is to keep going in the right direction. This is not about any final destination – it is about having a happy journey. I choose the happy journey now by focusing on the positive aspects of my world today.

Affirmation 60

I Set Fun Goals for Myself Each Month.

"Without a clear-cut, positive goal, set at the outset,
the situation just seems to happen, and makes no sense
until it has already happened." – ACIM

AT THE START OF EACH MONTH I sit down and make a list of goals for the month so that the Universal Mind has something to work with. If I don't do that, then ego co-opts that power and starts going to work on achieving fearful goals. We are not to be passive people on this earth. We are creators.

Make your goals fun for you. Don't set the goals you think you "should" want – set the ones that sound fun to YOU.

There is a dynamic Something in the Universe that responds to my thoughts, words, beliefs and attitudes. I use it wisely and consciously by directing my faith toward positive goals. I am a co-creator with my Source as I vision a month full of joyously unfolding good.

As I imagine and envision the best, the best is attracted into my world and I am happy to let my imagination soar into the Possibility Matrix where all things are possible for me. I am limited only by my capacity to imagine and receive – and today I am living beyond all limitation.

AFFIRMATION 61

I GIVE UP ALL SELF-CRITICISM.

"Do not dwell on the imperfection of yourself or others. To do so is to impress the subconscious with these limitations."
— NEVILLE GODDARD

I AM MADE IN THE IMAGE AND LIKENESS of the Infinite Creator. *No mistake that I have ever made, and no failure of mine, has changed the Self that God made whole and spiritually perfect.*

From this day on I refuse to criticize myself in my thoughts or words. I know that I will make mistakes, but I intend to learn from them as I surrender them to the Holy Spirit to heal so that I can be gently taught how to make a better choice in the future.

God does not love me for anything that I do or achieve – does not punish me for any failures or mistakes. There is no way to be a disappointment to the Mother-Father God for Source has infinite patience with me. But even as I accept myself now, I also yearn to grow more fully into the person that God would have me be. I enjoy learning how to expand my heart and my mind and I no longer compare myself to mythical and stressful ideals of perfection.

I release myself and I release all others to our unique perfect path in this life that we may enjoy walking together without attack, guilt, blame or shame. I now choose to see the good in myself, and the good in all others as I let go of any sharp, hard, or critical nature.

I love and accept myself just as I am – and I am willing to be changed by God in whatever ways would be helpful.

AFFIRMATION 62

I ALLOW MYSELF TO FEEL GOOD TODAY.

"A man is just about as happy as he makes up his mind to be." – ABRAHAM LINCOLN

WE CANNOT GIVE WHAT WE DON'T HAVE. I cannot share peace and joy if I have none myself. Abraham Lincoln suffered with crippling depression for long periods of his life so he is not giving out meaningless platitudes or coming from a shallow understanding of the human condition. As he took responsibility for his own emotional journey, so must all of us if we are to be everything that God created us to be.

The Universe is a friendly joyful Force, and happiness is my Divine Inheritance. I choose to activate happiness within myself by focusing on all that increases my joy. It is not selfish to make myself feel good. No one else is responsible for making me feel good. Even God cannot make me happy – that's MY job. I cannot activate joy in anyone else if I am not joyful. Therefore, I know that nothing is more important than that I feel good today. I choose the thoughts that uplift and soothe me as I massage my thoughts to better and better feeling places. Abundant good surrounds me and I choose to live this day in gratitude and appreciation.

Nothing can stop or hinder me from making the best of things. Each uplifting thought I have attracts more thoughts like it – and as I feel good, I am attracting good!

AFFIRMATION 63

THE BETTER IT GETS, THE BETTER IT GETS.

"When it rains, it pours." – ANONYMOUS

"THE BETTER IT GETS, THE BETTER IT GETS" is a way of keeping the mind focused on whatever there is to bless today – in the same way that saying *"the worse it gets, the worse it gets"* is a way of cursing our own lives. It is really about momentum and focus – because for most of us there is a choice each day of focusing on the things that we feel good about, or focusing on the things we do not feel good about. If we put most of our attention on what is going wrong, we are activating the energy that sucks other things into that same energy pattern. If we focus on what is going well, we are activating that energy, and other things can begin to get pulled along into that energy pattern.

The better it gets, the better it gets. I am looking forward to seeing just how good my life can get today!

AFFIRMATION 64

THE UNIVERSE DELIVERS MY GOOD TO ME.

"If we would only understand that God is not some far-off Deity; not a stern judge, but the beneficent force that we recognize as Nature – the Life Principle that makes the flowers bloom, and the plants grow; that spreads abundance about us so lavishly." – VENICE J. BLOODWORTH

GOD IS. Beyond this we cannot really say. We can see the evidence of God's Universe as we tap into that Presence and allow ourselves to release the resistance that comes from trying to control the universe. We can rest in the knowledge that God is, and that the Divine Principle that makes planets revolve around the sun can handle our lives with ease, joy, peace and beauty if we will only give up our ideas of struggle and sacrifice. As we learn to guide our thoughts and feelings, we can live by the power of attraction, rather than promotion – by Grace, rather than by bargaining.

The Universe has not lost my file and knows exactly where I am and how to make the most joyful use of me while taking wonderful care of all my needs with enough left over to share and to spare!

AFFIRMATION 65

LOVE LIGHTS MY WAY.

*"There is no battle that must be prepared; no time to be
expended, and no plans that need be laid
for bringing in the truth."* – ACIM

TRUTH IS. Because of this, there is nothing to defend or
protect. Only untruth needs defending. Even the ego thought
system is nothing more than a puff of smoke, a cloud that
temporarily obscures the sun and sky, which have remained
exactly as they have always been. Therefore, we can open
our hearts to Life today and let love lead the way. Fear not -
be not afraid. The battle is not ours and there is nothing to
fight. What a wonderful day to practice loving whoever is in
front of us today – and all that means is to think kindly
towards them and give them a break, even when they are
acting less than lovable. Whatever we give out, cannot fail to
be reflected back to us. Ideas do not leave their source.
Remember, sometimes we do not act very lovably either –
and what a miracle it is when we can cop to it and love
ourselves anyhow.

*I love to love. All around me today are opportunities to
join together in the peace, grace and joy of God. Instead of
focusing on where we do not agree, I will focus on common
ground. Instead of seeking special love and special
circumstances, I will look with kindness at everyone,
including myself. Love is lighting my way today and this
makes my heart smile.*

AFFIRMATION 66

I HAVE DIRECT ACCESS TO MY SOURCE.

"And the Lord came, and stood, and called as at other times, Samuel, Samuel. Then Samuel answered, Speak; for thy servant heareth." – 1 SAMUEL 3:10

MEDITATION IS THE WAY TO HEARING the still small voice within. HOW you choose to meditate is your own personal business – or whether you even call it that. You can simply think of it as "tuning in" or listening. But the point is that we all have equal access to God, to Source, to the Higher Self, to Infinite Wisdom.

Our kind of meditation has a purpose beyond all the wonderful benefits of relaxation and stress reduction. The purpose is to activate the peace and joy of God within, while marinating in the Divine Presence. And it doesn't matter if you get there by sitting on a cushion, walking on the beach, gardening, riding a bike, petting the cat, or working on your car. It's about tabernacling with the Universe – and all have equal direct access to the Prime Creator.

Here I am Lord, show me Your love. I offer my thoughts, words and actions, my hands, feet, and voice to You today. Speak to me. Heal my mind. Make joyful use of me. I'm listening. I'm available.

Then quiet your mind and actually listen for the still small Voice within to guide you.

AFFIRMATION 67

AS I CHANGE MY THINKING, I CHANGE MY LIFE.

"The only way to change your conditions in life is to change your mind about life." – VENICE J. BLOODWORTH

THE COURSE COUNSELS US TO *"seek not to change the world but choose to change your mind about the world"* as a way of renewing our minds. The greatest changes are changes in our own Consciousness rather than the endless effort of trying to control outer conditions. And the wonderful fruit of a change in our inner-self is that conditions usually begin to fall into their right order without manipulation and struggle.

I am willing to change my mind from every limiting belief to ones that affirm Life and joyous possibilities. I love learning to think more uplifting and soothing thoughts, not to change my life, but to change my experience of life. And the better it gets, the better it gets.

AFFIRMATION 68

I ALWAYS PREPARE FOR THE BEST OUTCOME.

*"If one asks for success and prepares for failure,
he will get the situation he has prepared for."*
– FLORENCE SCOVIL SHINN

ON MY BATHROOM MIRROR I'VE POSTED A STICKER that reads, *"What are you preparing for?"* As I am getting ready for the day, I need to be reminded to set my mind in the proper direction. Many of us gird our loins for a stressful day by thinking of traffic, moody co-workers, anxiety-producing appointments, regrets from yesterday, and so on. And we are setting ourselves up for misery even if none of these things happen – because they are already manifested instantly in our minds. We are living it now.

Better to prepare ourselves for what we WANT instead of what we dread or don't want. As you brush your teeth or wash your face you can begin to prepare for a day of effortless unfolding good by mentally visioning yourself in a state of peace and equanimity as you move through your day.

All things are held perfectly in the hands of God today as I walk through the world in joy and peace, expecting good to unfold before me in wonderful and delightful ways.

Affirmation 69

Life Loves Me & Love Pursues Me!

*"God is the Giver and the Gift and now creates
His own amazing channels."*
— Florence Scovil Shinn

So many spiritual and religious systems and schools of thought have made an enemy of the world and of life itself. We are taught that life is something we have to conquer somehow and that struggle is the normal state of being for humans. Many religions teach us that we have to do a sales pitch to some reluctant God in the sky in order to secure our good. We're taught to believe that the world is a harsh hard place to be and that it is out to get us.

But the spiritual Truth is that we are good, God is good, life is good and the world is good. There is only a stream of well-being. New Thought is founded on the knowledge that there is no evil; there are not TWO powers in the Universe, but ONLY God, only good. All appearance of evil comes from the insanity of believing insane thoughts and acting on them. All attack is a form of at least temporary insanity.

The sane thought is that Life is FOR us and that good is ours to accept and to experience in abundance. We need do nothing to earn or deserve our good for it is our Divine Inheritance. All we need to do is dissolve the old beliefs in struggle and suffering. And that is done one thought at a time – with patience and kindness toward self.

Life is my loving companion today as I walk through a friendly Universe that is always pointing me in the direction of the doors that are opening to my greater good.

AFFIRMATION 70

I RELEASE THE NEED TO BE RIGHT.

"Do you prefer that you be right, or happy?" – ACIM

BEING RIGHT IS OFTEN THE BOOBY PRIZE IN LIFE. I remember reading an interview with a celebrity who had just had a bitter breakup. In the interview he said that he would *"rather be lonely than wrong."* He is someone that you see in the press all the time getting into skirmishes with paparazzi or into fights on social media. He has a tremendous amount of "moral outrage" over HIS idea of what life, people and the world should be like.

Insisting on having our way, on being acknowledged as right, in having others see our point, in winning the battle, in having the last word, in setting others straight and correcting everyone – well, this tends to leave us depleted emotionally, physically and spiritually. More than that, it *does* tend to leave us lonely and separate in our self-righteousness.

There is another way. When we can quietly state what we think from a place of non-attachment to the outcome, we begin to experience the peace of God within us. And sometimes this even means saying nothing at all – giving up the habit of trying to "correct" everyone around us all the time with our "know-it-all" helpfulness. Sometimes a silent blessing toward those we disagree with is the fastest route to a miracle for everyone concerned.

Today I align myself with the Great Corrector of all errors. I resign from policing others and focus on letting God joyfully use me as I let go of thinking I have all the answers. I happily & humbly let Spirit lead the way.

AFFIRMATION 71

I OPEN TO RECEIVE THE GIFTS OF THE UNIVERSE TODAY.

*"Infinite Spirit, open the way for my immediate supply,
let all that is mine by divine right now reach me,
in great avalanches of abundance."* – Florence Scovel Shinn

YOU ARE A DIVINE CHILD OF LIGHT. You were not born to suffer, struggle and live a life of stress and anxiety. ALL that the Father-Mother Creator has is yours, but the question is, how open are you to receive it?

A "get" mentality is based on ideas of scarcity and lack. But a receptive mentality is based on the knowledge that the Universe is abundant, friendly and extremely generous to all who can soften enough to allow in all there is to receive.

The sun and rain are given to all who simply step outside to receive them. No one needs to earn them or deserve them. They are given freely and fully. This IS the abundance Principle of Life. Life loves you and is available to you, but only to the degree that you can receive it. A thimble will only hold a thimbleful of water. A bucket will only hold a bucketful of water and so on. Throw open the portals of your soul today! Open your arms wide and say,

I open to receive the gifts of the Universe today! I expect the right doors to open for me and to find friendly faces and loving people everywhere I go. I am the beloved child of a friendly Universe and all that I need is here for me as I continue to expand my mind, open my heart and line up with my greater good! I am the grateful co-creator of a most joyous and successful life.

AFFIRMATION 72

I ALWAYS HAVE WHAT I NEED.

"If one holds himself, whatever present conditions may be, continually in the thought of prosperity, he sets into operation forces that will sooner or later bring him into prosperous conditions." – Ralph Waldo Trine

RIGHT WHERE YOU ARE, GOD IS. The Infinite Source has not lost your file and is not busier with bigger issues than your individual life. EVERYONE is priority #1 to the Source, which is omnipotent and omnipresent.

Aligning yourself with the INFINITE resources of the Universe is not greedy and takes nothing from another person. We have a very difficult time grasping the concept of INFINITE GOOD, which is never depleted, for we tend to focus on "just so many pieces of the pie to go around." This is limited human thinking and has nothing to do with Who you really are and what is possible for you when you align yourself with a Source that never runs low.

Today is another opportunity to access your Divine Inheritance by reminding yourself Who you are and WHO created you. You were created to THRIVE, prosper and grow AS an extension of Source energy. It is the Father's GOOD PLEASURE to GIVE you the Kingdom! Open to receive it today by reminding yourself that all that you need is always available to you when you remember the Truth.

I give God pleasure today by receiving all the gifts this day has to bring to me. I am allowing more joy and good than ever before – more than enough to share and to spare.

AFFIRMATION 73

I EXPECT AND ACCEPT THE BEST.

"Consider the lilies of the field, how they grow; they toil not, neither do they spin: and yet I say unto you, that even Solomon in all his glory was not arrayed like one of these."
– Matthew 6:28-29

WHAT YOU EXPECT, YOU ARE MENTALLY PREPARING FOR - and much of this has to do with who and what you believe you are. What if you decided to expect the best every day and actually mentally prepared for it? We subconsciously create and attract the life we *think* we deserve.

Of course "the best" is very subjective and YOU get to decide what that means to YOU. What the world considers the best may simply have to do with popular opinion about externals. For instance, who decided that carnations are less beautiful and less desirable than orchids or roses?

Only YOU can decide what is the best in your world. Free yourself from the tyranny of the pop culture and what it tries to dictate, as you become the authority of what is good, and beautiful and worthy – and start with yourself. With no effort at all, you are the perfect you as long as you are being authentically yourself. There is no need to struggle or strive to prove your worth or deservingness. Expect the best because you ARE the best, created by the Best!

Mentally prepare yourself for a day of effortlessly unfolding good that reflects the beautiful creature you are.

Today I expect and accept the best as a reflection of God's perfect love for me. I release any need to struggle or strive as I joyfully walk through the open doors to my good.

Affirmation 74

I Am in the Divine Flow of Life.

"Magnetism is not generated; it is displayed. Health, wealth, beauty and genius are not created; they are only manifested by the arrangement of your mind – that is, by your concept of yourself. The importance of this in your daily life should be immediately apparent. The basic nature of the primal cause is consciousness. Therefore, the ultimate substance of all things is consciousness." – Neville Goddard

We are either aligned with the Divine Flow of life, or we are resisting it. When we are focused on fear, negation, lack, and general negativity, we are denying and resisting the Divine Flow and we are magnetizing all that is in alignment with that lack and negation.

The answer to this is quite simple; relax and go with the flow. It is not necessary for us to CONCENTRATE on what we want to magnetize into our lives. The law of attraction works without force or effort. We do not force gravity to work – natural laws don't need our "help" to work.

Of course relaxing goes against most everything that we've been taught about creating a good life. Yet the Truth is that as we let our minds relax, we are able to get into the positive flow of life and we are often effortlessly carried downstream to where there is more and more good already manifesting before us. Our real work is the orderly arrangement of positive thoughts and attitudes for consciousness to use as the source of our magnetism.

As I gently relax into the Divine Flow of life today, I am attracting all the best of everything into my world.

AFFIRMATION 75

I AM A MAGNET TO MONEY AND PROSPEROUS IDEAS.

"Take this statement: 'The unexpected happens, my seemingly impossible good now comes to pass.' This stops all argument from the army of the aliens (the reasoning mind." – Florence Scovil Schinn

WANTING MONEY IS NOT DIFFERENT OR LESS "SPIRITUAL" than wanting love, peace, joy, work you love, health, a baby, a happy marriage, enlightenment, or anything else. "Spiritual" types tend to prefer the word abundance, because of their fear and judgments about poor innocent money. Cash is neither cold, nor hard – it is simply a form of energy exchange. It is as neutral as electricity, which can be used to light and heat a home, or to electrocute and kill.

The important thing is to use money wisely as a servant and not as a false god. But this is true of everything. We get into trouble when we make a job, a relationship, a healthy body, or anything else the source of our good.

I have found that having money is not only fun, but it also provides me with the freedom to do my work without worry or sacrifice. In fact, most of the affluent people I know are extremely generous and are making a positive difference in the world, while enjoying their money. Money doesn't control them; they wisely use their money, by making friends with it. If you have judgments about money or wealthy people, today is the day to let all that go.

This is a prosperous Universe and I have made friends with money and wealth. I am a wise steward of the abundance that is flowing to me now. I am a magnet to money.

AFFIRMATION 76

I MAKE ALL MY CHANGES WITH LOVE & PATIENCE.

"The first step in the 'renewing of the mind' is desire. You must want to be different before you can begin to change yourself. Then you must make your future dream a present fact. You do this by assuming the feeling of your wish fulfilled." – Neville Goddard

I USED TO BULLY MYSELF INTO MAKING POSITIVE CHANGES. And of course it never lasted for long. Self-criticism and judgment is not how we create lasting positive change. It took me a long time to realize that I could love and accept myself and still want to make positive changes in my life and in myself. We can change ourselves with love and kindness.

It all begins with desire and a vision. In this way I am not getting rid of something or running away from anything – I am moving toward a more expanded idea of myself and of what I am capable of accomplishing and living.

It's been a nice gradual process over the years. It's a sorting out of what is helpful and valuable, and what is not. Perhaps you desire to be kinder, more patient, wiser, calmer, or any number of positive changes. The first step is to KNOW THAT IT IS POSSIBLE FOR YOU. Begin there and then start to IMAGINE yourself in that scene already. Imagine what it FEELS like to already have the qualities or to be living the new behaviors that you desire. You have the Power of the Universe flowing through you – direct it with your Divine Imagination and watch how it begins to unfold.

I allow myself to dream the dreams that soothe and uplift me as I evolve, grow and embrace my ever-expanding Self.

AFFIRMATION 77

I AM CALM AND CENTERED IN GOD.

"In other words, be true to your own soul, for it is through your own soul that the voice of God speaks to you. This is the interior guide. This is the light that lighteth every man that cometh unto the world. This is conscience. This is intuition. This is the voice of the higher self, the voice of the soul, the voice of God." – Ralph Waldo Trine

HOW WONDERFUL TO REMEMBER that not only is God not far off, but that God is *"closer than breathing, nearer than hands and feet"* to us. We are not alone, nor bereft of help today or any other. It is more a question of whether we have made the connection or not. This connection is quite easily made because it isn't made at all – it is acknowledged as already so; it is remembered and affirmed.

We are centered in God because there actually is nowhere else that exists. We cannot be apart from God today anymore than a wave can be separate from the ocean, or a sunbeam from the sun. We are never alone or separate.

So take a moment now to acknowledge this loving infinite connection. Let your shoulders drop, relax your jaw and eyes, take a deep breath and say to yourself quietly,

I am calm and centered in God. There is nothing for me to do or fix or change today to make this so. I have all the Help I need today to walk in perfect peace, and Grace and love. I release all fear and resistance, knowing that God goes with me wherever I go and that even now, the right doors are opening for me to walk forward into my greater good. All is well in me and in my world today for I am not alone.

Affirmation 78

There Are No Limits on Me or on the Law.

"The more you think about this law, the deeper you will see it goes. It hands you a blank check, signed by the Maker of Universal Law, and leaves you to fill in the amount – and the kind – of payment you want!" – Gardner Hunting

Greed is not good, but it is misunderstood. There is nothing greedy about deciding what you want to get out of life, or even in deciding that you WANT to get more out of life. There is nothing greedy about living a life of luxury if that brings you joy and you find it fun. Greed is wanting good to be exclusive to you or to the chosen few – not for anyone and everyone. Greed is ULTRA limitation thinking. It is the extreme opposite of a win-win consciousness.

And true generosity is not giving everything away to others. True generosity is not hoarding anything, but it is also the abundance consciousness that wishes prosperity and success for all. It is a spiritual state of being which allows that there is enough good to go around and that our giving does not diminish our own resources for we have a limitless Source that supplies and fills every need.

Are you limiting yourself based on your age, background, the economy, your body, your abilities or lack of them, your current job, what science currently teaches, where you live, your education and talents, your sex or sexuality, the beliefs and biases of the culture, or anything else? If so, today is the day to dissolve those lies with Truth.

I am the limitless child of an abundant and generous Universe. I was created to live, thrive and succeed TODAY!

AFFIRMATION 79

MY WORLD IS A REFLECTION OF MY CONSCIOUSNESS.

"Your patience with your brother is your patience with yourself. Is not a child of God worth patience?" – ACIM

CAUSE AND EFFECT IS A FUNNY THING. It takes some practice to learn how to connect the dots in our lives because we tend to look for an EXACT reflection in the form, but it is often not like that for us.

For instance, John may not understand that the reason he cannot find and keep a job is because of his judgments about people with weight issues. He may not see the simple cause and effect of it.

His attack thought of, *"Fatties are just lazy people who won't stop stuffing their faces full of food! It's so easy to just go to the gym and eat right."* And that person with the weight issue may say, *"Why can't John get and keep a job? It's so EASY to just show up and do your job and keep it, unless you are lazy and stupid!"* In both cases, there is a lack of compassion and acceptance – and what we cannot accept is a spiritual lesson that will be repeated until we finally pass the class. If you have no compassion and acceptance for those you've judged, you'll also have none for yourself when YOU fall down and have trouble getting up.

My friend, author and teacher Debbie Ford used to always say, *"What you can't be with, won't let you be."* Try to practice non-resistant compassion & acceptance today.

I release everyone, including myself, from my expectations of perfection. I practice compassion and understanding toward all others and myself as I open my heart to the peace of God.

AFFIRMATION 80

MY MISTAKES AND FAILURES DO NOT DEFINE ME.

*"The Holy Spirit is not delayed in His teaching by your
mistakes. He can only be held back by your
unwillingness to let them go."* – ACIM

GROWTH IS OFTEN HUMBLING and sometimes downright embarrassing. I don't know anyone who grows and spiritually matures in a straight line forward. We tend to zig and zag quite a bit along the way. Backsliding and messing up is to be expected on this journey of *"progress, not perfection."* The point is to learn from those mistakes – to not make excuses for them, but to forgive and release them.

When we start to try something new we are vulnerable and not sure-footed. It takes time before we are proficient at staying out of debt, keeping the house clean, managing our moods, keeping our word, being sober, being compassionate, or whatever it is you are currently working on. What matters most is getting back up when we fall down – without punishing ourselves or shutting down.

Where you are is perfect for today. If you've fallen down, see what there is to learn from the situation, WITHOUT BLAME, GUILT OR SHAME, and then get back on the road. Don't think of it as starting over – think of it as part of the journey. If there is any real gift in falling down, it's that it can help us to be more compassionate and kind to those around us when they fall down and mess up. We're all attending Earth University and all around us are fellow students who need our helping hand.

I see my mistakes as opportunities to practice self-love.

AFFIRMATION 81

I REST IN THE PEACE OF GOD TODAY.

"If I defend myself I am attacked . . . And it is this you do when you attempt to plan the future, activate the past, or organize the present as you wish." – ACIM

THE COURSE IS NOT REALLY AGAINST OUR MAKING PLANS or being organized – what this quote is about are the deeper motivations and Consciousness we are coming from when we do anything. It is asking us to let go of the FEAR that is often behind our planning and organizing – the fear that gives rise to defensiveness and self-protection. Basically this boils down to our ATTACHMENT to our plans and organizing rather than the plans themselves.

When we practice trusting the wisdom of Spirit within us we will still make plans and organize things, but from a place of peaceful non-attachment to outcomes. We understand that by aligning with Source BEFORE we do anything, we are releasing our need for things to turn out a certain way. We are not afraid of the world anymore. We know that if we align ourselves with Spirit first, and then our plan still falls apart, that there is something better coming along, even if it is still farther down the path. We trust. We are on a "need-to-know basis" much of the time.

To rest in the peace of God IS to trust that regardless of appearances, God has not abandoned us or lost our file. If we will hang on the Vine and continue to affirm the best, every storm will pass and we will come out unscathed.

I trust the Peace of God within me to lead and guide me to my greater good as I release attachment to outcomes today.

Affirmation 82

All the Treasures of Life Lie Before Me Today!

"Realize today that there is no poverty in nature; there is poverty only in the human mind! When you break the mesmeric hold that negative thinking about wealth has on your mind, you will be able to come into any part of the universal storehouse of riches that you choose for your very own. No one may keep you from your God-given destiny buy yourself!" – Anthony Norvell

Poverty begins in the mind. Poverty is a belief in lack, whether it is poverty of time, money, love, energy, health or anything else. Therefore, true abundance begins in the mind as well. In fact, the days and nights we live are lived primarily in our own mind - in our consciousness.

The Universe is an Energy of limitless abundant creation of more, more, more and we are a part of this Universal flow. It is up to each of us to go to the well of Living Waters every day to withdraw what we choose to. We can come to the Well with a thimble, a bucket, or a barrel. Our Consciousness is the container for how much of the limitless good we will receive each moment. Our daily work is the gentle expansion of our capacity to allow greater and greater good into our experience – enough to share and to spare!

Today we can awaken from the hypnotism of the world that tries to keep us small and afraid. There is nothing to fear for the Universe is seeking those who are ready for more.

The Divine Plan for my greater good is now joyously and easily unfolding before me in perfect timing and in delightful ways. I expand to receive all that Spirit has for me today.

AFFIRMATION 83

I CAN CHOOSE MY OWN DOMINANT VIBRATION.

"Deep within you is everything that is perfect, ready to radiate through you and out into the world. It will cure all sorrow and pain and fear and loss because it will heal the mind that thought those things were real, and suffered out of allegiance to them . . . The way will be open, if you believe that it is possible." – ACIM

WHATEVER WE BELIEVE, OUR MIND SETS OUT TO PROVE. Mind is always proving itself right by gathering up evidence that is in agreement with whatever it already believes. The mind is very loyal in this way. It is on the side of whatever we believe to be true – even if we are wrong. This is why when we change our beliefs we change our own world.

Everything is energy – everything is vibration. We are vibrational beings in a vibrational Universe. Our dominant vibration on any particular subject is simply what we currently believe about that subject. The good news is that when we change our beliefs, we are changing our vibration, and it is vibration that attracts or repels in our energy field whether for the better or for the worse.

If we believe that life is hard and no one likes us, then mind will gather up lots of evidence to prove that case. If we believe that life is good and we are blessed then mind will gather up evidence to prove that case. We are lawyer, judge and jury of our own lives. Which case will you prove today?

I choose to activate beliefs that bring more joy, peace and love into my awareness today. I believe that life is good, I am good, and the world is good. I choose to be happy today.

AFFIRMATION 84

I RELEASE THE NEED TO CONTROL.

"I do not perceive my own best interests." – ACIM

OUR HIGHER SELF SEES LIFE from the Broader Perspective. In our humanness we only see through a glass darkly – we register only the tip of the iceberg. Therefore, we cannot really judge what is happening in our lives since we don't know where it's all leading. Letting go requires trust in God.

In my own life, I've noticed the paradox of how often what I thought were my worst humiliating failures led to the greatest experiences of my life. And certain dazzling shiny dreams coming true showed me that there was nothing there but cheap tinsel, emptiness, struggle and sorrow.

When we get attached to having things turn out a certain way, it creates fear and resistance within us. This fear and resistance usually kicks us into the "control mode" where we are endlessly trying to fix, change and manipulate ourselves and the world around us. We become attached to the form rather than the content. We think that living in a certain city is the ONLY way for us to be happy. That we MUST be married, or own our own business, or have our body look a certain way, or have a certain reputation in the world in order to be happy. And we are quite frequently wrong, wrong, and wrong about these things. So the Course quietly asks us, *"Do you prefer that you be right, or happy?"*

I gladly surrender to my Higher Self today, to the greater vision for my life. I tune in and listen to the Guidance of Source and I gently follow my intuition without attachment to any outcomes. I trust the Universe to work it all out.

AFFIRMATION 85

I WITHDRAW MY FOCUS AND ATTENTION FROM FEARS, REGRETS AND WORRIES.

"A plant will remain visible for some time after its roots have been cut, but it will gradually fade away and eventually disappear; so the withdrawal of your thought from the contemplation of unsatisfactory conditions will gradually, but surely, terminate these conditions." – Charles F. Haanel

TURNING AWAY FROM CONDITIONS is something that is greatly misunderstood in New Thought circles. Too often it is assumed to mean that we ignore bad news or push down and suppress our feelings. This is NOT what we mean.

What we do is take whatever sensible action there is to take about the eviction notice, the cancer diagnosis, the job loss, the breakup and so on. We calm ourselves as best we can, go within, and seek Divine Guidance, which we then FOLLOW. I usually suggest that people also write out all their fearful negative thoughts on paper and then at the end, surrender them to God and make a new list of how they WANT to feel.

But, once we have done that, we withdraw our attention from fear, regret and worry – and we begin the process of making positive affirmations about the situation, and everyone and everything involved in a way that feels good. We begin to turn toward the Consciousness of the answer instead of turning toward and chewing on the problem.

I am one with the power that creates Universes, and I turn to that Power now to heal, soothe and solve every problem in my world. I have consulted the Higher Authority.

AFFIRMATION 86

MY CONFIDENCE IN MYSELF IS GROWING DAILY.

"The process of rising from your present concept to a higher concept of yourself is the means of all true progress. The higher concept is waiting for you to incarnate it in the world of experience." – Neville Goddard

WHAT WOULD YOU DO IF YOU WEREN'T AFRAID? Whether we want to admit it to ourselves or not, we are goal setting and goal-achieving creators of our own experiences. Some of our goals are conscious, and others are set by default through the thoughts that we think and by what we believe and expect out of life.

I was filled with terror when I left Pennsylvania in my early 20's. I had hopes and dreams but barely a kernel of confidence in myself. Thankfully, a kernel is all it takes to begin a journey to the fulfillment of our dreams. I took that kernel and put my faith in it as I went forward toward my Divine Destiny, even as I sometimes trembled with fear and even broke out in hives from nervousness. I kept on going forward, and each step forward put another brick in the foundation of my belief in myself. Often, we must DO the thing BEFORE we have the confidence. And it is the doing, which builds the new self-concept.

Achievement of our dreams and goals has far less to do with circumstances, talent, and potential than it has to do with how much we believe in ourselves – and how much we are willing to walk through our fear and resistance one step at a time. Confidence grows AS we consistently take action.

I am becoming more of my whole fabulous self every day.

AFFIRMATION 87

I GIVE MYSELF PERMISSION TO THRIVE AND SHINE!

"Fortune waits upon you. Seize her boldly, hold her – and she is yours. She belongs rightfully to you. But if you cringe to her, if you go up to her doubtfully, timidly, she will pass you by in scorn. For she is a fickle jade who must be mastered, who loves boldness, who admires confidence."
– Robert Collier

THERE IS A GENERATIONAL DIFFERENCE that I've noticed which I think that those of us who are older may need to take a look at so that we can learn from those who are coming up behind us. Boiled down, I would simply call it boldness and a lack of timidity. There is a whole generation of people who, for better or worse, are not afraid to ASK for what they want and to put themselves out there in big ways.

Taken to the extreme this can come out as narcissism or an unhealthy self-obsession, or a sense of entitlement. After all, this is the age of "selfies" and keeping nothing private or discreet. But some of us of an older generation were taught too much of the opposite – to sit down and shut up, to not take up too much space, to wait until you are asked, to apologize for existing or having needs.

As usual, what is needed is a nice healthy balance. We can all learn from each other, and in fact, this is why opposites attract. It is a way of the psyche seeking balance. So, perhaps there is some area of life where you have been holding yourself back or playing small and timid – and this your time to let that go as you boldly seize the day.

I am not afraid to go for my dreams and ask for what I want.

AFFIRMATION 88

I SPEAK MY DREAMS AND VISIONS INTO REALITY.

"So shall my word be that goeth forth out of my mouth: it shall not return unto me void, but it shall accomplish that which I please, and it shall prosper in the thing whereto I sent it." – Isaiah 55:8-9

WORDS ARE POWER VESSELS. The words we speak are creating our experiences every day, all day long. We live the life that we are describing with our language and conversations. We can talk something up, or we can talk it down. We can talk ourselves into greater good – or we can talk ourselves out of it.

Years ago I got tremendous pleasure out of telling self-deprecating stories and entertaining people with my sarcasm, and stories of terrible dates, humiliating experiences and my many failures in life. In fact, for years people in my classes would call me a "spiritual comedian." It took me a long time to break that habit and I still have to be conscious of it today because many of us joke ourselves out of our good all the time while entertaining others. It's not a coincidence that so many comedians suffer from deep depression.

"When you laugh at yourself, you are singularly likely to laugh at others, if only because you cannot tolerate the idea of being more debased than they are. All of this does make you feel tired because it is essentially disheartening. You are not really capable of being tired, but you are very capable of wearying yourselves. The strain of constant judgment is virtually intolerable. It is a curious thing that any ability which is so debilitating should be so deeply cherished." - ACIM

I speak positively about myself and others today. I talk myself into greater good with every word I speak.

AFFIRMATION 89

THE UNIVERSE LOVES ME AND IS CONSPIRING IN MY FAVOR.

"The optimist is right. The pessimist is right. The one differs from the other as the light from the dark. Yet both are right. Each is right from his own particular point of view, and this point of view is the determining factor in the life of each. It determines whether it is a life of power or of impotence, of peace or of pain, of success or of failure." – Ralph Waldo Trine

IF WE KEEP DOING WHAT WE'VE BEEN DOING, we'll keep getting what we've been getting out of life. One of the foundational purposes of New Thought is to get more out of life. And the way we get more out of life is by putting more into it. We are seeding life with our thoughts, attitudes and actions – and they will bear fruit, bitter or sweet.

Someone once said, *"You can live 90 years, or you can live the same year 90 times."* Quite a difference there, don't you think? I am very much a creature of habit and this is great when the habits are positive and bear good fruit. But when they aren't good, it's up to me to change them – to try a different route, another way, to shift my perception and habits. I used to have a victim mentality even in my spirituality and I walked around with a lot of fear and worry. It's been a long and rewarding journey in turning that around in my Consciousness. Now, I not only bless the new day ahead, I walk home from the gym thanking the trees, the grass, the sidewalks, the sky, the cars – everything, for doing their job so beautifully. And I've noticed how it's increased my good! I'm on the radar of the good stuff. Change is good. I've made friends with the Universe – anyone can.

The Universe is my loving partner. We're a great team.

AFFIRMATION 90

I BOLDLY TAKE ACTION ON ACHIEVING MY GOALS AND HAVING MY DREAMS COME TRUE.

"Until one is committed, there is hesitancy, the chance to draw back – concerning all acts of initiative, there is one elementary truth that ignorance of which kills countless ideas and splendid plans: that the moment one definitely commits oneself, then Providence moves too. All sorts of things occur to help one that would never otherwise have occurred. A whole stream of events issues from the decision, raising in one's favor all manner of unforeseen incidents and meetings and material assistance, which no man could have dreamed would have come his way. Whatever you can do, or dream you can do, begin it. Boldness has genius, power, and magic in it!" – Goethe

I CAN'T REALLY SAY IT BETTER THAN GOETHE DID, though apparently much of the above quote did not come from him anyhow. What matters is the Truth of it. There is no power in being wishy-washy about our dreams and goals. Too often people "spiritualize" themselves out of being proactive and decisive. I think this comes from past experience of being stressed out over having goals, or feeling awful about any "failed" dreams. It's a sad attempt to keep disappointment and stress at bay and then calling is spiritual.

It's what some teachers call *"the will to fail"* in which we fail by talking ourselves out of even taking the first step. This can be over some huge dream, or even something as small as attending a party or saying "hi" to a stranger. It's a misguided commitment to staying small. Let's not do that.

Each step I take gives me more courage and confidence in myself and in my dreams. I am bold and determined to win.

AFFIRMATION 91

WONDERFUL OPPORTUNITIES AWAIT ME AS
I GO FORTH IN AN ATTITUDE OF CALM DELIGHT.

"Sometimes you are tempted to follow the reasoning mind, and argue with your intuitive leads, then suddenly the Hand of Destiny pushes you into your right place; under grace, you find yourself back on the magic path again. You are now wide awake to your good – you have the ears that hear (your intuitive leads) and the eyes which see the open road of fulfillment."
– Florence Scovel Shinn

THE REASONING MIND IS A WONDERFUL GIFT and a very necessary and helpful tool in this life. But I have found that quite often the best experiences of my life were nothing I could have ever reasoned out with my own mind. They came from my turning within and seeking the guidance of my intuition, which is the result of our connection to Infinite Mind. They came when I was not struggling or striving to figure things out – at times when I'd stepped back and focused on rest or play. In fact, many of the greatest scientific discoveries in humankind were made when the scientists were relaxed and not even thinking about the problem they were trying to solve.

Much of our modern world has been moved forward scientifically, medically, artistically and in every other way in moments when answers or insights just seemed to "drop" into the mind or awareness of the discoverer. We can become finely tuned conduits through which good comes forth into the human storyline and condition.

All the answers I need come to me as I relax and tune into the Divine Mind. The path before me is lit by miracles.

AFFIRMATION 92

THE UNIVERSE MAKES JOYFUL USE OF ME TODAY.

"Remember the parable of the talents. You know what happened to the man who went off and hid his talent, whereas those who made use of theirs were given charge over many things."
– Robert Collier

HOARDING ANYTHING GOES AGAINST NATURE and blocks the flow of our ever-expanding good to and through us. Too many people are waiting for a "job" to organize their talents and energy for them before they will start pouring forth their energies. Or they are miserly about truly giving at the job they have because they don't think THIS is where their true talents lie and so they are resisting truly giving their all.

When I began teaching back in 1985, not only did I not make any money at it, for the first 5 years or so I was in the red because I never broke even at anything I did. I would set up for a seminar that NO ONE attended – and I still had to pay for the rental of the room and whatever I spent on supplies. But I felt inside that I was priming the pump and that if I just kept on allowing the Universe to flow through me to help others, I would be led and guided to and through the right open doors. In the meantime, I worked at a lot of secretarial and retail jobs that paid my rent and allowed me to keep pouring money into following my dream.

Now, 30 years later I am making a very good living but I still start every day of my life with the prayer, *"Here I am God, make joyful use of me today"* and then I open up and let the energy flow through me.

As I am joyfully used by Source, I am blessed and prospered!

AFFIRMATION 93

AGE IS NOTHING BUT A MEANINGLESS NUMBER.

*"In youth we are constantly growing. We KNOW we have not yet
reached our prime. We know we can expect to continually
IMPROVE. We look forward to ever-increasing physical powers.
We look forward to a finer, more perfect physique. We look
forward to greater mental alertness. We have been educated to
expect these things. Therefore, we BELIEVE we shall get them –
and we GET them! . . . You can keep on growing more perfect,
mentally and physically, every day. Every minute you live is a
minute of conception and rebirth."* – Robert Collier

YOU ARE NEITHER TOO OLD NOR TOO YOUNG. In Truth, we
are ageless, timeless, immortal non-physical beings that
sometimes become physical for a while. Age is really mostly
a matter of caring *"what the neighbors will think"* about
what you are being, doing or having at this time in your life.
How old would you be if there was no one around to witness
you and no cultural mythology to tell you what is or isn't
appropriate at your age? How different might your choices in
life be if you had no idea how old your body is?

The world is obsessed with age, but you do not have to
be. You can free yourself from the belief that age is anything
other than a meaningless number. There are some cultures in
which the people <u>don't even know</u> how old they are. They
do not count days, weeks or years and in fact have no words
for "time" or the "when" of anything. They live in the now.

Artist Beatrice Wood, who was active until she passed at
age 105, was asked about her longevity and she replied, *"I
owe it all to chocolate and young men."* Atta girl.

I am an ageless outrageously expanding being of Light!

AFFIRMATION 94

I HAVE WHAT IT TAKES TO REACH MY GOALS.

"Every habit and faculty is preserved and increased by correspondent actions, as the habit of walking, by walking; or running, by running." – Epictetus

YOU MUST REALIZE THAT YOU HAVE WHAT IT TAKES to live the life you choose and to realize your dreams. Too many of us have a habit of talking ourselves out of things that we would do better to talk ourselves into. We let fear stop us from stepping out there and continuing to grow and learn and risk, in spite of hurts and failures of the past.

Most of this comes down to mental habit patterns. We get into a pattern of stopping ourselves or we get into a pattern of encouraging ourselves. We get into a habit of playing small or we get into a habit of going for it.

Knowing this, we can begin to change any negative limiting mental habit patterns – we can turn them around and make them into empowering affirmations that encourage us to go for it. But what solidifies a mental habit pattern is taking the corresponding ACTION that grounds the new thought into our conscious and subconscious mind. Words are extremely powerful, and yet nothing is cheaper than talk. I can say I love you all day long, but if I am never there for you, break my agreements with you, take advantage of you, and ignore you, then our relationship will not bear good fruit. I have to SHOW UP and follow through with my thoughts and words. We have to know that within us is whatever we need in order to push through and succeed.

My confidence is growing as I take positive action every day.

AFFIRMATION 95

I AM WORTHY BECAUSE I EXIST.

"Your worth is not established by teaching or learning. Your worth is established by God . . . Again, - nothing you do or think or wish or make is necessary to establish your worth." – ACIM

"I AM LOVABLE BECAUSE I EXIST" is a fantastic affirmation that I learned listening to Louise L. Hay many years ago and it still rocks me to this very day.

Many of us grew up with the stressful concept that we must justify our existence through our hard work and struggle – that our worth comes from our accomplishments and that just "being" is never enough. We become obsessed with self-improvement without ever asking; *"who is this "self" that we are always trying to fix or change in some way or other?"*

It's wonderful when we make positive changes in our lives or in our selves out of a feeling of love. Sometimes we have a desire to drop old destructive or negative habits and replace them with more loving positive ones. That's a beautiful thing. But if we are doing it out of a sense of self-loathing and hatred, then quite often we find that no amount of improvements will ever quite do enough. We will always find ourselves lacking in one way or another and the finish line just keeps moving – we're never any closer to arriving.

Peace comes from realizing that the real self is the spirit within us, which is already totally lovable and loving – it's the self that God made as an extension of God. Therefore, we can love ourselves as a creation of the Divine, right now.

I am worthy and lovable simply because I exist. I am enough.

Affirmation 96

I Run My Own Race.

"The ego literally lives by comparison." – ACIM

At no other time in history have we known more about what other people are being, doing, having and experiencing at this exact moment, even if they are living across the world from us. Thanks to social media we can see into the lives of millions of total strangers with just the touch of a finger.

It's very easy then to get caught up in judging ourselves and everyone else according to appearances. We can judge our worth on how many "likes" or "followers" we have. It's as if the whole world has become a giant high school popularity contest. But we all know that what is most admired or popular may or may not have any real merit.

Hitler was extremely popular and had countless followers who were all highly organized and well dressed. He was an early expert in "branding" and defining a mission with logos and catchphrases. On the other hand, Jesus had about a dozen scruffy followers who argued amongst themselves, seldom followed directions, and were often unclear about what or how to do anything. Jesus had a rather awful team and He was terrible at branding or at galvanizing a movement. On Sunday the people had a parade for Him as He rode into town on a borrowed donkey and by the next weekend they wanted Him crucified. He would have sucked at social media and yet His message lives on thousands of years later for any who have ears to hear it. He did not compete or sell; He simply ran His own race.

Life is not a popularity contest. I came here to do me full out.

AFFIRMATION 97

THERE IS A DIVINE PATTERN FOR MY LIFE.

"In back of every thing is the One Thing." – ERNEST HOLMES

LET US TODAY THINK NOT IN TERMS OF A DIVINE PLAN for our lives, but instead think in terms of a Divine Pattern. The Divine Pattern is the invisible, in back of the visible. It is the spiritual pattern from which the physical can be formed, much like a dress pattern for a dress or a blueprint for a house. Behind the pattern is the Designer or the Architect.

One Mind wrote every song, sings every song, writes every book, dances every dance, and creates every creation. We are creative beings because we are extensions of the One Creator – and we co-create by tapping into the Infinite Intelligence in order to channel the Creative Flow.

Healing then is realignment with the Divine Pattern. There is a Divine Pattern for a healthy heart, a clear mind, a harmonious relationship, a fulfilling career, a prosperous bank account and for a happy life. The Divine Pattern is restored as we align ourselves with the One Thing in back of every thing.

As we relax and tabernacle with the Divine Presence, we are returned to alignment with the Divine Pattern which is then individualized in and as us. Each of us are unique expressions of the Divine Pattern, therefore the Pattern is really not one of uniformity but of evolving and expanding creation. Therefore, we can celebrate all the differences within us and others instead of trying to "fit in" or demand that others change. We are all the multi-colored threads in the Divine Tapestry.

I celebrate my uniqueness today for I am a Divine Creation.

AFFIRMATION 98

I CHOOSE AND ACCEPT THE BEST IN LIFE.

*"I am an irresistible magnet, with the power to attract unto myself
everything that I divinely desire, according to the thoughts,
feelings, and mental pictures I constantly entertain and radiate. I
am the center of my Universe. I have the power to create whatever
I mentally choose and accept. I begin choosing and mentally
accepting the highest and best in life. I now choose lavish
abundance for myself and for all mankind. This is a rich friendly
Universe and I accept its riches and hospitality now."*
– VETURA PAPKE, PRACTITIONER OF PRACTITIONERS

I FIND THAT MORE AND MORE PEOPLE HAVE COME to see that
quantity of life means very little without quality of life.
There is a whole "tiny house" movement in which people are
deliberately downsizing their "stuff" in order to enjoy their
lives now rather than delaying their joy until the day they
possibly retire. That is just one way that people are choosing
to create a life that focuses on quality of living each day.

True prosperity and wealth are not about the
accumulation of dollars and things but rather about living
from a place of choosing and accepting limitless possibilities
for our good. In fact, "hoarding" is considered a mental
illness that requires serious psychological help now. Of
course there is nothing wrong with having as many things as
you like as long as it does not feel burdensome or cause you
to constantly delay your joy.

The essence of New Thought is getting more out of Life,
by recognizing that Life is generous and friendly.

*I recognize myself as a limitless being with limitless
resources at my disposal. I line up with my abundant good!*

AFFIRMATION 99

THE DOORS TO HEALTH, WEALTH, LOVE, JOY, PEACE, LOVING COMPANIONSHIP AND HARMONY OPEN BEFORE ME TODAY AND I WALK THROUGH THEM WITH EASE.

"You see what you expect, and you expect what you invite. Your perception is the result of your invitation, coming to you as you sent for it. Whose manifestation would you see? Of whose presence would you be convinced? For you will believe in what you manifest, and as you look out so will you see in. Two ways of looking at the world are in your mind, and your perception will reflect the guidance you have chose." – ACIM

WE CHOOSE, EITHER DELIBERATELY OR BY DEFAULT, what guidance we will accept each day, in every moment. We either let the voices of fear and limitation lead us - or the still small Voice of love, limitlessness and inspiration guides us.

Life is not happening to us. Life is responding to our vibration and our Consciousness. Recognizing this is where the point of power begins. We erroneously think that we must strive, struggle and work hard to live the good life, but in Truth there is no need to earn our Divine Inheritance – but we do have to BOLDLY step up to receive it, expecting that it will be freely given because we are only asking for what is already ours. We must BELIEVE that we are worthy to receive the gifts of the Kingdom in order for the gates to open up for us.

Whatever we expect today we are literally inviting into our experience – and the doors to what we expect will open before us. What doors are you expecting to open for you?

I expect & accept the best today. As a Child of the Universe I gratefully accept today's portion of my limitless good!

Affirmation 100

I Don't Have to Have All the Answers.

"I do not know what anything, including this, means. And so I do not know how to respond to it. And I will not use my own past learning as the light to guide me now." – ACIM

We have immediate access to a Limitless Source of wisdom, power, love and Grace. Sometimes in our fear and arrogance we believe that we are being called upon to always know exactly what to do or say in order to have a happy outcome for ourselves and everyone involved. This is an extremely stressful way to live.

Usually what upsets us most is not what happened in a particular situation but rather the meaning we have assigned to what happened. If someone leaves us, we may think that means we are not good enough, or that relationships are difficult, or that it says something about men or women. It is often the meaning we assign that tends to cause us the most suffering. We bully ourselves with our perception of things.

What if we decided to give ourselves a break? What if we took a step back, took a deep breath, and relaxed into the space of not knowing? If we are willing to release our need to immediately UNDERSTAND everything, we can then open up to a wisdom that is beyond our past learning and the fearful voices of the world. Grace happens when we are willing to humbly step back and let Spirit guide us.

I relax into Grace today, knowing that as I open my mind to the Beloved Infinite Spirit I am guided and led through even what I do not understand. I rest in God today as I step back and let Source lead the way. There is nothing to fear.

AFFIRMATION 101

I AGREE TO LEARN WITH JOY AND TO
TRUST THE PROCESS OF LIFE UNFOLDING BEFORE ME.

"The opposite of joy is depression. When your learning promotes depression instead of joy, you cannot be listening to God's joyous Teacher and learning His lessons." – ACIM

A GREAT LIE OF THE WORLD is that our deepest growth comes from hard life lessons of loss and suffering. I believed that one for a very long time and can now say from experience that the only real lesson that suffering offers is the realization that you don't want or need to suffer.

In fact, joy is a much deeper teaching which offers more variety and limitless growth and expansion. The dark is just . . . dark. It is LIGHT that has all the colors and variations of the spectrum. There is no limit to what we can learn by exploring the light. It goes on and on and on.

In 2005 I decided to begin to learn through joy instead of pain. This is a great mental discipline that requires much more work than the laziness of just letting the mind sink into darkness and negativity. At first, it seems like an awful lot of work to choose to continually focus the mind on light. But then you realize that though it is easier to bitch and complain about everything, it is also much more exhausting and debilitating in the long run. And so, though my body is a decade older than when I started this practice, I feel younger and lighter all the time. Joy IS truly the fountain of youth.

I look forward to the joyful lessons before me today. I know that Life loves me and that everything is unfolding in perfect order and timing for my greatest good. I am a joyful learner.

Notes

Jacob Glass is an author, spiritual teacher, mentor and international supermodel. To order his other books, see his live class schedule or receive his weekly class recordings, see his website: www.jacobglass.com

CPSIA information can be obtained
at www.ICGtesting.com
Printed in the USA
FSOW01n1328050117
29280FS